TRENCH ■
Warrior

RON PEGG

CREATION
HOUSE
PRESS

This heartwarming account of the journey of a family committed to doing things God's way will be an inspiration to all who read it. Written by a faithful man about a faithful family, this is the type of story that reinforces good feelings about good people.

It is a breath of fresh air at a time when many works are trying to correct situations; this one just shows a situation that is just right, including its own trials. Read it and get refreshed!

—Tommy Barnett
Senior Pastor, Phoenix First Assembly

It is said that one person can make a difference, but have you ever wondered if your life really counts? Ron Pegg's *Trench Warrior* encourages each person to continue to fight the good fight of faith every day. Whether the world is watching or not, what you do is recorded in heaven, and every step of faith is taken in victory. This story tells of one man's fight, his refusal to let his adversary overtake him and his trust in the orders of his Commanding Officer. This book will inspire you to keep fighting the good fight!

—Lloyd Zeigler
Director, Master's Commission

As Ron Pegg's pastor, I found this book to be very interesting. It tells the story of the tradition of faith in a long line of Peggs that dates back to the Quakers in the 1600s. This is a family that has stood for its belief and practiced what it preached in so many areas of community life.

Ron has been a beacon of light for his family, friends, school, neighbors, church, various sports and community. His love for God is obvious, and his love for humankind is expressed in his mission to the community and beyond. He has been a support and mentor to many people, including myself. You will enjoy reading about the life story of a man totally committed to his Lord and Savior.

—Martin Garniss
Flesherton Pastoral Charge
United Church of Canada

TRENCH WARRIOR by Ron Peg
Published by Creation House Press
A part of Strang Communications Company
600 Rinehart Road
Lake Mary, Florida 32746
www.creationhouse.com

Unless otherwise noted, all Scripture quotations are from the Holy Bible, New International Version. Copyright © 1973, 1978, 1984, International Bible Society. Used by permission.

Scripture quotations marked NKJV are from the New King James Version of the Bible. Copyright © 1979, 1980, 1982 by Thomas Nelson, Inc., publishers. Used by permission.

Scripture quotations marked KJV are from the King James Version of the Bible.

Scripture quotations marked NLT are from the Holy Bible, New Living Translation, copyright © 1996. Used by permission of Tyndale House Publishers, Inc., Wheaton, IL 60189. All rights reserved.

Library of Congress Catalog Card Number: 2001088037
International Standard Book Number: 0-88419-780-8

01 02 03 04 05   8 7 6 5 4 3 2 1
Printed in the United States of America

DEDICATION

This book is dedicated to my dad and mom,
who lived as trench warriors their entire lives.

And to Mrs. Hazel McCague,
Mr. and Mrs. L. O. Thornton,
Mrs. Selby Dobbs,
Mrs. Harold Ellison and
Mr. Harrison,
all of whom were influences in the life
of this trench warrior.

And to my wife, Cathy,
who has always stood shoulder to shoulder with
me throughout our lives in the trenches.

CONTENTS

INTRODUCTION

In lands across Western Europe, much of World War I was fought in a style called trench warfare. For more than three years, the people in the trenches lived and fought on both sides of the barbed wire and no-man's land. Few advances were made. There was little retreating.

In a small space in the trench, a person fought, ate, slept, saw rats, caught lice, seldom bathed or changed clothes and saw people wounded and maimed for life. They often received wounds themselves, and sometimes in that small space, death was the end.

Many of us live a life in Christ that appears to have many characteristics of the life of a warrior in that trench. There is no fame. The person a mile down the trench doesn't even know our name and often doesn't care, or so it seems. And yet the trench warrior served a major purpose in World War I.

This story shows a portion of the life of one of the Lord's trench warriors. Yes, the trench warrior for the

Lord does have a purpose. Above anything else, a trench warrior lives to His glory.

> For our light affliction, which is but for a moment, worketh for us a far more exceeding and eternal weight of glory; while we look not at the things which are seen, but at the things which are not seen: for the things which are seen are temporal; but the things which are not seen are eternal.
>
> —2 CORINTHIANS 4:17–18, KJV

CHAPTER 1

THE ROOTS

Great is the LORD, and most worthy of praise, in the city of our God, his holy mountain... Walk about zion, go around her, count her towers, consider well her ramparts, view her citadels, that you may tell of them to the next generation. For this God is our God for ever and ever; he will be our guide even to the end.

—PSALM 48:1, 12–14

The Pegg family, a hard-working, industrious people who went about their own business, had lived in the Norfolk area of Eastern England for many centuries. When the Quaker movement began to influence that part of England in the 1600s, many became members. They followed the teachings of prayer, meditation and being peace-loving people.

In the mid-1600s, Oliver Cromwell, famous for his massacre of the Irish at Drogheda, became the leader in

England. Cromwell did not understand the Quakers. He did not understand meditation and the desire and need for continual prayer. Above all, Cromwell had no toleration for anyone who was not prepared to go to war. As a result, the Quakers in England were persecuted by Cromwell and his followers. Many of the Peggs left England and traveled across the ocean to the New World—America. They settled in the area that would become Pennsylvania. History records that when William Penn arrived in this area, he stayed in the first house that had been built in Pennsylvania, a house built by Daniel Pegg.

After a century of living in the New World, a number of Peggs found it necessary to pack up and leave their land. The reason was the American War of Independence. These people did not claim to be British Empire Loyalists. Still followers of the Quaker faith, they did not fight for the British, but they also did not fight for American independence. Their neighbors, who were fighting for independence, did not understand. They thought that if these people were not fighting for American independence, they must be part of the enemy. And that's how they were treated. When the persecution by their neighbors and government became too much, the Peggs traveled by wagon trains across New York state to the Canadian border at Niagara Falls. It was a long, hard trip.

After reaching Canada, the Peggs settled just north of Toronto in East Gwillimbury Township, just east of Newmarket.

The year was 1804. My great-great-grandfather, Samuel Pegg, made this trip as a twelve-year-old walking behind his parents' wagon. The families had just settled in this area when the War of 1812 broke out between England and the United States. The two countries were fighting for control of Canada. When the Quakers, recently arrived from the United States, did not join the war, their neighbors became suspicious. But, the Canadian characteristic of tolerance became evident at this early time in its history. The war passed, and the Quakers stayed.

A short time later, Samuel and his wife, Nancy, moved ten miles east to develop a homestead in Scott Township near Uxbridge. In those days, ten miles was greater than two thousand miles today.

Samuel and Nancy Pegg found themselves cut off from the Quaker groups. Those were the days when the Methodist circuit rider preachers were traveling around the settlements of early Ontario. The preacher would come and spend a few days in one settlement, then move on to the next, returning in two or three months. Samuel's family became members of this group, which was influenced greatly by Charles and John Wesley.

It was on this homestead that my father, Garnet, was born sixty years later. From here he would go to the little Hartman Methodist Church, where my mother, Pearl Boden, also attended. In this church, my grandfather, Thomas Boden, was Sunday school superintendent, and my mother's grandfather, Emmanuel Brown, who had immigrated from England, was the guest speaker on a number of occasions, as he ministered for the Lord as a lay preacher.

When the Methodist church joined with the Presbyterian and Congregational denominations in

1925, the recently wed Garnet and Pearl Pegg would become members of the new United Church of Canada.

Within a few years, the Peggs moved with their two young daughters, Bernice and Marion, more than thirty miles away to Beeton, where Dad joined his brother in the baking and grocery business, of which Dad had little knowledge.

In 1931, a third daughter, Norma Jean, joined the struggling family.

CHAPTER 2

DAD AND MOM

Honor your father and your mother, so that you may live a long time in the land the LORD your God is giving you.

—EXODUS 20:12

Bernice was fifteen; Marion was eleven; Norma soon would be seven. It was 1938. That's when I was born. I was supposed to be born March 6, my Grandma Boden's seventieth birthday. I arrived in time for breakfast, March 7. One of the characteristics that I have been labeled with throughout my life is that I am seldom, if ever, early. I arrived into this world seven hours late and have been trying to catch up ever since.

The year 1938 was the end of the Great Depression and the beginning of World War II. Many of my first thoughts and experiences were of the war and the Depression. My brother, David, was born a little less than two years later to complete our family.

My father and mother quickly would become the two most influential people in my life. My mother had become a person who did not enjoy life outside of her own home nearly as much as she did at home. Her life was wrapped up in her husband and five children.

Mother seldom went to church because she didn't like being associated with many of the people there. On the other hand, she was an amazing theologian. She had grown up in Thomas and Harriet Boden's family of nine children. When her younger sister died of the flu in 1917, Mother became the youngest. She adored and respected her father and mother, who passed on to her a love for God's Word.

On a Sunday morning, Mother would be up before 7 A.M. with her radio in the kitchen. She would listen to one gospel message after another, taking a break to make sure her children were up and off to Sunday school at Trinity United. She also made sure that we went about our preparations quietly. We were not to disturb our father, who slept after six busy days in the baking and grocery business. This included a Saturday that began before 8 A.M. and ended just before midnight, when the last customer left our grocery store. Father usually attended the regular church service at Trinity, which was at 7:30 Sunday night.

After getting her family off to Sunday school, Mother would tune in to the Churchill Tabernacle in Buffalo, New York, where Clinton Churchill was minister. When we returned from Sunday school, dinner, as we called it, was ready.

Mother would then spend two to three hours on Sunday afternoons listening to more gospel broadcasts. On Sunday evenings, most of the family would be gathered in front of the radio listening to such favorites as Henry Aldrich, Jack Benny, Amos 'n' Andy, Edgar Bergen and Charlie McCarthy, as well as Fred Allen's *Allen's Ally*. Mother would listen awhile. Then she would disappear into the kitchen to her radio, hoping to pick up the evening program from the Churchill Tabernacle.

When I was born, my mother wanted to call me Clinton after the pastor that she so admired. However, a hero from one of the books she had read was named Ronald, so that's what Mother named me, to go along with Lawrence, her favorite brother's name.

My father never talked about theology or, for that matter, Christianity. He was supportive of my mother and our family. When I was a small boy, I believed my dad was perfect. He could do no wrong. This idealization was fed by my mother, who created the image that Dad was king of her castle.

Meals were served when it was convenient for Dad. They were prepared with Dad's tastes in mind. If there was an extra piece of pie, Dad had first refusal. Mother ran the house; Dad ran the bake shop and the store. They respected each other's boundaries of authority. Mother accepted my dad's spiritual headship, even though she had much more knowledge and understanding of the subject.

When I became old enough, I often would go with my dad to church on Sunday nights. *The Jack Benny Show,* Dad's favorite show, was on the radio from 7 to 7:30 P.M.

We would listen to it until the beginning of the last commercial. Then we would leave on our five-minute walk to church, arriving during the first hymn. I often wonder why I went. Dad would give me one of his pens and pencils that he carried in his three-breasted suit. By the time the minister started preaching, I had already taken the mechanical pencil apart and put it back together many times and was restless. Almost as soon as the sermon began, I would put my head on Father's lap, and the next thing I knew, the service was over.

By the next Sunday night, I was ready to go with my dad to relive the experiences.

I have always been thankful that there was no kindergarten when I was growing up. During those years, my dad was on his bread and grocery routes five or six hours a day, five days a week. During the year I would have been in kindergarten, I spent the days with my father as he delivered his orders. Dad always had one of his special cookies for every child on the route. Sometimes a friend, Eddie Crocker, and my brother would go with us. Dad would allow us to travel on the running board of the truck, or he might drop us off at a creek for a few minutes while he delivered up a side road. Although the owners of most of these farms have changed, I could almost go from farm to farm and recall the names of most of the people on his routes.

CHAPTER 3

EARLY MEMORIES

And Jesus grew in wisdom and stature, and in favor with God and men.

—*Luke 2:52*

One of my favorite games was pretending that I was a radio preacher. I would get the piano stool, wind it up high, place a broom upside down in front of it and place a couple of hymn books and a Bible on the stool. The stool was my pulpit, and the broom was my microphone. I would conduct a service with songs, Scripture and a brief message. I had been dedicated as a small child in the traditional United Church method of sprinkling, which is accepted as baptism in many churches.

Like all five-, six- and seven-year-old kids, I went to Mission Band once a month. There we always sang:

> Jesus loves the little children
> All the children of the world
> Red and yellow, black and white
> They are precious in His sight
> Jesus loves the little children of the world.
> —Public Domain

The Presbyterian church in our village of seven hundred had a boys group called Trail Rangers. My friends and I joined the group of fifteen with Rev. Duke in charge. The theme verse of Trail Rangers was Luke 2:52: "And Jesus grew in wisdom and stature, and in favor with God and men." As part of the program, we spent a few minutes each week studying the Bible. It was there that I came to know John and Peter MacPherson better than I had before. The MacPherson boys made it clear that if Trail Rangers was held in the United Church, they would not come. Their family was one of the many that had maintained a Presbyterian denomination when the United Church was formed. The MacPhersons considered the United Church evil. It was good when United Church boys came to Trail Rangers in the Presbyterian church building. In their opinion—and many others'—the reverse was not possible.

When I was eight, Grandma Boden fell and broke her hip. My mother, brother and I went to her home for a couple of weeks to look after her. Grandma's eyesight also was failing. One day, Mother suggested I read to her from the Bible. When I asked Grandma if she would like me to do that, she said she would like me to read from the Psalms, her favorite book of the Bible.

I had my first visit to the People's Church in Toronto when my dad took us to hear Mother's favorite guest speaker, Clinton Churchill. This was also my first direct contact with Oswald Smith, the founder of the People's Church.

Mrs. Dobbs was our Sunday school teacher. The Sunday school class was taught around the sink in the church's kitchen. Mrs. Dobbs didn't have the greatest control of the class of nine- and ten-year-old boys. Mrs. Cecil Reynolds assisted her. I do not remember any of the Sunday school lessons Mrs. Dobbs taught except the one she taught by example at Christmas. She had the whole class to her small house for a Christmas party. The boys were boys. We did not deserve the party, but that wasn't the reason she had it. She showed us her love by having us in her home. Love is the reason for the season.

Miss Wallwin, who was nearly eighty years old and the teacher of the adult Bible class, would sing along with us before we went to class. Those of us standing directly in front of her would have a hard time keeping a straight face. Miss Wallwin was a beautiful lady, but she could not sing. She was an early lesson from God. Scriptures do not say sing a beautiful, right-on-key, per-fect-pitch tune unto the Lord. Scriptures say, "Make a joyful noise unto the Lord." Rejoice!

I was around ten years old when Pastor Hall began coming to our village on Sunday evenings and holding service in the Orange Hall. Few people went. I attended regularly. When Mr. Hall offered gospel plaques for vis-itors, I brought people. On one occasion, it was my dad. On another occasion, it was my mother. The service at our church, Trinity United, was now held in the morning, not that it mattered much because I always went to Sunday school but seldom stayed for church.

It was at the Gospel Hall services that I came to love such songs as "Whiter Than Snow," "Showers of Blessings" and "There's Not a Friend Like the Lowly Jesus." I bought one of the hymn books that they used.

When Pastor Hall held tent meetings the next summer, I went. But his congregation did not grow, and my attendance became more irregular. He soon stopped coming to our village.

It was not until almost thirty years later, when I was looking through the hymn book I had bought, that I came to realize that Pastor Hall was my first exposure to the Pentecostal teachings of God's Word.

Vera Hastings came into my life in fourth and fifth grade. What a change she made. Miss Hastings gave marks for each day's work. I suddenly went from the lower half of the class to the top part. I received many awards from her, including my first real Bible. It was a prize for a good mark. When I completed fifth grade, I learned that Miss Hastings would be leaving. On the first morning of summer vacation that year, I lay in my bed bawling like a baby because she was leaving.

CHAPTER 4

THE LAST YEARS OF INNOCENCE

You then, my son, be strong in the grace that is in Christ Jesus. And the things that you have heard me say in the presence of many witnesses entrust to reliable men who will also be qualified to teach others. Endure hardship with us like a good soldier of Christ Jesus.

—2 TIMOTHY 2:1–3

My dad had suffered from severe headaches for many years. He had heard about David, a boy who was a faith healer. He was coming to Rochester, New York, for some services. Dad decided to go. But we had too many family members to fit into our truck, so I was chosen to go with Dad and Mom, while my brother, David, would stay home and help Norma look after the store and keep her company. We were to leave for Rochester at 4 A.M. Dad had gone to the garage to get the truck. When he left, Mother got down beside a kitchen chair, and I knelt down beside another. She suggested we pray for a safe trip and for Dad's healing. When we finished praying, we got into the truck and headed east out of the village. When we had traveled almost two miles, my Mother realized that she had forgotten her teeth. Dad turned around. We got the teeth and began our journey again.

Mother had remembered to pray but had forgotten her teeth. How many people would have remembered their teeth but forgotten to pray? It was what Mother was about–first things first.

We got to Rochester before noon and attended an afternoon service. People prayed for Dad. Dad said his headaches did not go away, but they became less severe.

On another trip, the whole family went to Buffalo to hear Clinton Churchill in his own church. When we were returning that Sunday evening, we stopped in Toronto to attend a tent meeting that Oral Roberts was holding. At the end of the service, Oral had his altar call. My brother and I raised our hands. We were then asked to stand. I didn't want to, but David insisted that we stand. We then went forward, and people prayed for us. The purpose of the altar call was so people could accept Jesus as Lord and Savior. That was the night David made his decision. But that was not the case for me. Going forward was an outward expression of a relationship I had with Jesus since I was a small boy. I do not know the day or hour this happened in my life. I just know that Jesus has been my Lord and Savior for as long as I can remember.

Dad had become the Sunday school superintendent,

a happy surprise for me. Dad was a go-getter. He soon had the Sunday school in two teams—one red and one green. The purpose was to see which team could have the best attendance during the next six weeks of classes. On the first Sunday, those present were evenly divided. Brother and sister were often on opposite sides. When someone new came, he would be added to his host's color. During the next six weeks, attendance rose 50 percent. The losing side had to make dinner for the winning side. Attendance did not stay at this level, but the competition created a lot of enthusiasm for Sunday school attendance.

Dad had been superintendent for a couple of years when he decided that I should be his assistant. I was glad to do it. Dad remained superintendent for three more years. When he retired, his plan was for me to be superintendent.

CHAPTER 5

THE END OF INNOCENCE

No one engaged in warfare entangles himself with the affairs of this life, that he may please him who enlisted him as a soldier.

—2 TIMOTHY 2:4, NKJV

While a member of Trail Rangers, I was elected secretary-treasurer. The next year, I was elected president. The year after that, another boy and I tied for president. Rev. Duke decided that the other boy should be president because he had never held that title. I would have thought he would go with experience but...

Peter Bell was always full of life and mischief. Everyone loved Pete. My brother and I, Pete and many other eleven-, twelve- and thirteen-year-old boys from

Beeton used to hitchhike out to a river called Sand Hook to swim in the summer. One Monday afternoon in early July, four of the boys went to Sand Hook. My brother and I could not go because our sister Norma was on holiday and we had to help in the store. On their way home, the boys were picked up by a local woman. They ended up in a head-on crash that killed the other car's driver. Eleven-year-old Pete died in the hospital. Another friend suffered a severe broken pelvis, another a broken collar bone, and the fourth a severe concussion. The driver of their car suffered internal injuries. But for the grace of God, my brother and I would have been in that car.

When I arrived at the secondary school level, I was nominated as the male athletic club rep for my class. Both boys and girls had a vote. Being the ninth-grade charmer that I was, I carried the boys' vote quite handily, but the girls all voted for another guy. He won.

In my sophomore year, I lost the vote for class rep. In eleventh grade, I don't remember running, but if I did, I lost. In twelfth grade (junior year), I was nominated for school executive. Everyone in school could vote for four candidates. The one with the most votes would be president, second would be vice president, third would be treasurer, and fourth would serve as secretary. There were seven candidates. I finished seventh but got the most votes in my class.

I remember hearing one of the boys from our class who obviously had not voted for me speaking to a friend in the hall. He said, "Can you believe Pegg got the most votes in our room?" I was overjoyed because those who knew me best had voted for me.

The End of Innocence

My brother was a sophomore, and a couple of his friends said they would not vote for me because I probably would hold Sunday school every day. This was the same year Dad retired as Sunday school superintendent. He did not attend the annual Sunday school meeting, expecting his son would be the new superintendent. It did not happen. A group of people in the church felt I was too young. When Dad discovered they had elected an older man, he was upset. He knew my plan was to go to college to become a minister, so he raised enough noise that the new superintendent resigned—and I got the job.

During the next three years, Sunday school attendance topped at 130 people—three times what it had been.

The new minister was not in my corner. I gave him an announcement about the Sunday school anniversary that stated the service would begin at 11 A.M. sharp. When he read the announcement in church, his comment was, "I do not know what the 'sharp' is about—11 A.M. is 11 A.M." Everyone knew whom he was chastising.

Meanwhile, another year had gone by at school. I had been chosen to represent our school at the Ontario Athletic Leadership Camp. While I was there, I preached my first sermon. It was based on the chorus "Dare to be a Daniel." The chorus goes:

> Dare to be a Daniel
> Dare to stand alone
> Dare to have a purpose firm
> Dare to make it known.
> —Public Domain

19

The sermon was short, but it was about the need to evangelize. Later in the summer, I spoke in our church. The subject was "If Baal be god, then follow him. If the Lord be God, then follow him." The sermon was well accepted. Later, my father told me he had a sermon prepared in case I didn't make it.

In the fall of my senior year (there were five years of secondary school in Ontario, Canada), I was elected school president. It was while I was in this position that I discovered that to lead, one has to serve. I spoke to most students in the halls of the school. I always chaired the clean-up committee after school dances. Because I had no girlfriends, I spent little time dancing at the school dance. I was often in discussions about Jesus Christ.

During that school year, I continued as Sunday school superintendent, I was president of our new youth group, I was busy playing hockey, I was coaching my third team, and I played in the school orchestra. While I originally learned to play the clarinet, when the school bought an oboe, I agreed to play it in the orchestra.

One weekend that spring, our orchestra played at another school. Our orchestra played a number of selections, and also played together with three other schools. I was the only oboe player. One of the pieces chosen for the mass orchestra featured the oboe. The concert was to be part of a radio presentation the next day. During the concert, I came in seven bars too soon. The orchestra was in chaos. Needless to say, that particular selection was not on the radio the next day.

The hockey team I was coaching that winter was a young, bantam team. On one occasion, I told my mother that I would rather the team win the Ontario championship than for me to pass that year at school. I did not pass. However, coaching hockey was just one of many reasons, which also included the class presidency, the youth group, Sunday school, playing hockey and the orchestra.

When I learned I failed the school year, I was not upset or discouraged. I believe it was God's will. I failed botany with a 34 percent. I had never failed that subject before and never would again. It is the only exam that I have ever written where I knew everything except the material covered by the exam. I failed zoology by three marks. One of the exam questions asked for the term for a single-celled animal. The second I stepped out of the exam room, the answer, *amoeba*, came to me. My other failure was Latin grammar. I passed Latin authors, but got only a 33 percent in Latin comp. Like botany, it was the only time I ever failed Latin comp. My writing skills have never been good, and at a later date, a school secretary said, "Mr. Pegg, it is obvious you do not teach penmanship. In fact, it's obvious you never took penmanship." Marie Banbrook, my Latin teacher of six years, felt the person who marked my exam was not impressed with my writing. Regardless of the reason, it was a one-time failure.

I prepared to return for my sixth year in secondary school. I would get the chance to coach the hockey team to a 24 and 0 record before entering the Ontario finals, where we lost three straight. I would begin two other hockey teams for smaller boys in our village. I would carry on as president of our youth group and superintendent of Sunday school, and I was re-elected for a second time as president of the Student Council. It was one of the greatest years of my life because I had time to be involved in all these activities. I only needed three subjects to graduate. I was able to pass them the second time around.

CHAPTER 6

INFLUENCES

Let the elders who rule well be counted worthy of double honor, especially those who labor in the word and doctrine.

—*1 TIMOTHY 5:17, NKJV*

Throughout my teen years, Mother continued to be the major influence in my life. She was always available, and she was my best friend. When I would come home from school, she was always there. We would talk about my day. We would talk about Jesus. She was my prayer warrior. She would pray for me while I was taking an exam or coaching a hockey or baseball team. She prayed for me when I was speaking in church or to a youth group.

Hazel McCague had come to town from Toronto. She had worshiped in the People's Church, one of the world's greatest missionary churches. She also had worshiped as a young person in Avenue Road Church, where Chuck Templeton had an outreach for Youth for Christ before eventually denying his faith.

Mrs. McCague became the teacher of our youth group. Every Sunday morning, we were challenged with the gospel of Christ. We were asked to give our lives to Jesus. This woman had a dynamic impact on our liberal church. She enhanced what my mother had always preached in our home.

At the same time, Mr. and Mrs. L. O. Thornton moved to our town. Their background was similar to Mrs. McCague's. I spent many hours visiting the Thorntons. He not only became my assistant Sunday school superintendent, but he also became my mentor. Mrs. Thornton could never get over Chuck Templeton's denial of his faith. He had been used of God to help thousands of people find Christ. He was considered to have had greater potential in the world of Christ than Billy Graham.

My Aunt Bertha was a different kind of influence. Aunt Bertha certainly believed in the letter of the law—or something similar. She was married to my mother's brother, Peter. Uncle Peter was a good Christian man, but like the rest of the Christians in this world, he was redeemed by the blood of Jesus, not his own righteousness. At seventy, he would periodically sneak away to the races. He was not allowed to visit his sister, who lived three doors down from him, because she might have the television on. He could not go across the street to visit my dad's aunt who was approaching ninety. She had two children who were about the same age as my uncle. Both were born handicapped. One never spoke a word during his seventy-plus years of life. The other had been taught housework, which she could do under her mother's supervision. My dad's aunt had spent her life looking after these two people, but sometimes a friendly game of Euchre would take place. My aunt did not want my uncle involved in such a game.

Irwin Joyce was like a big brother to me. His dad had worked for my dad for twenty-five years. Irwin often helped around the store and bake shop. He was the one member of his family who attended church. When Rev. Duke needed help with the Trail Rangers, he always would ask Irwin. Then Irwin went to work in Toronto.

In the fall of my junior year in high school, we got an unusual amount of rain. One Friday in mid-October, it began raining hard in the morning and did not stop. The streets in our village had streams running along the curbs. There was water in our basement, and by dinnertime, the water was almost up to the kitchen. We heard a report that five people were stranded in a car in Wilcox Creek. As a boy, that was one of the creeks I had often played in while traveling on my father's bread routes. The creek was not even big enough to fish in. But the reports proved to be true. Five people died in that stranded car. More than one hundred people in southern Ontario died in Hurricane Hazel that night. One of the victims was Irwin Joyce. He, too, died in Wilcox Creek as he was coming home from Toronto. He drove into the river that had been raging for five hours, and his car over-turned. His body was found the next morning a mile down stream, separated from his car. The rain had stopped around midnight, and the next morning, the creek was back to normal.

But why Irwin? Why? Why was such a fine young man allowed to perish in the storm? Why do bad things happen to good people?

The most amazing influence in my teenage years was the Holy Spirit. His influence is amazing as I look back because, although I was aware that the Holy Spirit was here, I was a long way from knowing His wonderful and unbelievable power. Of course, I was also unaware of His complete love and devotion to the Lord Jesus and to the Father.

I made most of my money as a teenager cutting grass. (Irwin Joyce got me started.) This meant that I could keep my own hours. It also meant that some weeks in July, I was almost out of business. In our house was an old pump organ and a piano. The two were beside each other. I used to spend hours playing the organ with one hand and the piano with the other, while my feet pumped the organ. It's not that I was a good player—I played the melody with both hands and often with two or three fingers.

It wasn't playing that was important. It was what I played. Hour after hour after hour, I would play the gospel hymns. I did not know the verse of scripture that says God inhabits the praises of His people. It was at least twenty years before I would become aware of this scripture.

Influences

The Holy Spirit was leading me because I was open to God's leading. There are many other scriptures that reveal that I was being led by the Holy Spirit in my undertakings, long before I had any real knowledge of those scriptures.

CHAPTER 7

BOB JONES UNIVERSITY

The devil said to him, "If you are the Son of God, tell this stone to become bread." Jesus answered, "It is written: 'Man does not live on bread alone.' "
—*LUKE 4:3–4*

Bob Jones University in Greenville, South Carolina, has as its slogan, "The world's most unusual university." Dr. Bob Jones was a great evangelist who eventually received an honorary doctorate degree when he founded Bob Jones University.

It was while reading information on Billy Graham that I first became aware of Bob Jones. Billy Graham was on my mother's radio in the late 1940s and early '50s. He became an early hero of mine. He had begun his university training at Bob Jones University, although

I did not know at the time that he had only lasted a couple of semesters there.

I came to discover that Bob Jones University had many students from Canada. One of Bob Jones' biggest supporters was Oswald J. Smith and the People's Church. In fact, the future pastor of People's, Oswald's son Paul, was a Bob Jones University graduate.

The school had a number of musical ensembles, which traveled about North America in the summer. The ensemble proclaimed the gospel and recruited students. I became one of those students. My father and mother assisted me in finding out all we could about Bob Jones University. My mother had heard Bob Jones on the radio when he preached in the People's Church and earlier at Buffalo's Churchill Tabernacle. She was an immediate supporter of my going.

This was 1957. I was a young boy from a village of seven hundred planning to go to a university in another country. I will never forget hearing Bob Jones preach at our first school assembly. He was saying that America had "gone to the dogs" and a major spiritual revival was needed. I was ready to head out with him to help take on the evils of America. It never happened. The 1960s came with its rebellion and "God is dead" theory.

Bob Jones University was extremely right wing. Some have said it was run like a military school. Dating could only take place with a chaperone. There was a six-inch rule in regard to contact with a member of the opposite sex. A student could not leave campus without permission. A date off campus had to be pre-arranged, and a chaperone traveled with those who were dating. Blacks were allowed to work at the school but were not accepted as students. The school believed that marriage between people of different color was against the will of God. It was not that blacks were inferior, but different.

I had been at Bob Jones University for a couple of months. One night, I was going to dinner with a couple of friends and a senior student. Because I didn't like spicy foods, I said I hoped they did not have chili that night. The senior student said, "You better be careful making a statement like that. You cannot criticize the school." I just didn't want their hot chili.

I was content at Bob Jones University as my basic faith as a Christian was growing. The foundation of my faith was secured. I was a preacher boy. The theme song was:

> *Souls for Jesus* is our battle cry
> *Souls for Jesus* we will fight until we die
> We never will give in while souls are lost in sin
> *Souls for Jesus* is our battle cry.
>
> —Public Domain

In spite of my outward happiness at that school, there was an underlying restlessness. I had become aware of Bob Jones and his close friends' disagreements with Billy Graham. I was also aware that Billy Graham's sermons were always based upon the Word of God. It was also evident that Dr. Oswald J. Smith, pastor of Canada's largest evangelical church, was not against Billy Graham. Years later, Mr. Graham would conduct Oswald Smith's celebration sermon when he went home in his nineties.

As a preacher boy, I had the experiences of being part of a team that led services in chain gang confinements, jails, Sunday afternoon children's Bible classes and Saturday night youth outreaches in auditoriums and on street corners. One of the places that we held Sunday afternoon Sunday school was on the front porch of an unpainted house. It was sitting on a half-dozen pieces of wood, so when it rained, the runoff would go under the house.

We sang the chorus:

> I may never march in the infantry
> Ride in the cavalry
> Shoot the artillery
> I may never zoom o'er the enemy
> But I'm in the Lord's army.
>
> —Public Domain

There were eight kids and two leaders on the porch. We sang the chorus with action. That made the entire house rock.

Then there was the first time I had the opportunity of speaking in the men's African American section of the jail. Unlike the white section, all the men came out to the front area, sat down and prepared to listen. My subject for the evening was "Except a man be born again, he cannot see the kingdom of God." One man had recently found Jesus as his Savior. Almost before I spoke my first words, he began to chant, "Amen." He never stopped until I stopped. I didn't know if anyone heard anything I had to say, but maybe God was using the "amen chorus" to inspire the rest of the inmates.

Bob Jones had many of America's top preachers of

the '50s come to the school. It was a great opportunity to hear the gospel. Often, however, following a guest preacher's visit, the most popular form of entertainment was to "roast" him. The question would inevitably be asked, "If he's a Christian, how can he say that?" The person asking the question would usually be referring to one short statement removed from the speaker's entire presentation. That was life at Bob Jones University.

At Christmastime, I was able to get a ride with four other students back to Cleveland, Ohio. From there I would fly to Toronto. Early in the trip, we began to discuss our vacation. My plans included going to a high school Christmas dance. One of the boys was immediately down my throat: "How could you possibly consider going to a school dance? That would be backsliding!" He never let up on me all the way to Cleveland. I went to the dance anyway. I was able to witness to at least a half-dozen students there.

I did not return to Bob Jones University after Christmas for many reasons. Up to that time in my life, BJU was the nearest place to heaven that I had ever experienced. But despite the positive aspects, I was not happy while I was there. Although I had said I was going to be a minister, I began to realize that it was more my idea than God's. People had been telling me for years that I should be a minister, but what was God saying?

The right-wing, self-righteousness of the university did not sit well with me. A few years later, Billy Graham held a crusade in Greenville, the location of the university. The students of Bob Jones University were told that they could not attend the crusade. If they did, they would be suspended.

CHAPTER 8

COMPLETE CONFUSION —ALMOST

So he, trembling and astonished, said "Lord, what do You want me to do?" Then the Lord said to him, "Arise and go into the city, and you will be told what you must do."

—ACTS 9:6, NKJV

What happens to a nineteen-year-old boy who has always known what he is going to do with his life and has always followed what he believes to be God's leading, but then things don't work out the way they were supposed to? In other words, what does one do when God doesn't seem to show up? It's always easy when God shows up. But what if He doesn't? Looking back, I now realize it's simple. First of all, God knows what He's doing, and it will all be for His glory. Second, wait—He will show up!

What was I going to do? Our church had honored me one night before I left. More than one hundred people had come to our Sunday school room to say good luck and give me gifts. I had already proved I was far from vulnerable by spending six years in high school. Besides, a small town is like a family. A family is often your biggest critic, but if you develop a problem, the family is with you all the way. That is the way it was in Beeton.

One of my friends said I was too young to have been that far from home. It was not long before I was teaching a Sunday school class and coaching two hockey teams. Before I had left, and this is probably the most important factor of all, my dad said to me, "Son, we are with you. We have researched the university. If it should happen that it is not what you think, please remember that there is always home."

My dad was in the process of retiring from his forty years in the bake shop and grocery business. I helped him with this. The Presbyterian minister and I had become good friends. There were vacant pulpits in the area, and he was the supervisor of a couple of these. He often had me speak on one of the three-point charges. I went into our grade school as a supply teacher on two occasions.

I did not wish to return to school. I believed I would never go to school again. I went to Toronto to the army recruiting office, where I spent a day filling out forms and taking tests. Upon my return the next day, I would be in the army. By God's grace, I did not go back.

Our minister thought I should become an official candidate for the ministry of the United Church. I went with him to Presbytery, where I was interviewed. Reverend Jim Shilton chaired this committee. During the questioning, he concluded that I was not ready to take this step. This was the first of many times that Rev. Shilton would influence my life.

Because there was a shortage of ministers in the United Church, it was suggested that I should apply to spend a year as a lay supply preacher. I did. At the end of June, I was to go to Cochrane in Northern Ontario to work with a six-point charge.

In the meantime, a number of interesting events took place. I met a young person on the streets in Alliston who was graduating from high school and was going to attend Waterloo University College. I was not aware of a college in Waterloo. One of my concerns about going to school was that all the Canadian universities that I was familiar with were in big cities. I didn't want to go to a big city. Waterloo had twenty-two thousand residents with a college enrollment of just more than four hundred students. I was not going back to school, so this did not matter. Two weeks later, I was invited to lunch by a family in Bradford that attended the Presbyterian church where I was speaking. A young man at lunch said he went to Waterloo University College and that this school could be an answer for me—but I was not going back to school.

One of the jobs that I did in the village was reading the electrical meters for Beeton Hydro. At Miss Willoughby's house, the meter was in the basement. After reading her meter, Miss Willoughby, a retired school teacher and a member of the Beeton School Board, asked me how I enjoyed teaching the couple of days that I had supplied. I told her it was fun. She said, "I suggested to the Board that they ask you to supply. I thought that if you taught a couple of days, you might decide to become a teacher." I thanked her. I did not tell her what I was thinking: *Lady, I will never be a teacher!* The Saturday arrived that I was to head to Cochrane for my year's work as a lay supply minister. My dad had helped me buy a new Volkswagen, and my mother had packed a lunch for me. As I got into the car to leave, Dad said, "Well, Son, you are finally getting to do what you want to do." I could not tell him what was in my heart. My heart was saying, "No, Dad, it isn't."

I drove the eight hours to Cochrane and arrived late in the afternoon. I was met by Alex and Ruth Taylor, who were leaving to go to Holstein in Southern Ontario. They had been on this charge for a couple of years. Alex was going to Holstein so he could attend school to get his bachelor's degree and, at the same time, serve as a student pastor. What school was Alex going to attend? Waterloo University College.

On Sunday morning, Alex took me around to meet people at the various churches while he said good-bye. He and Ruth were to leave for Holstein after lunch. Alex asked me if I would mind taking a boy to church camp in Timmins on Sunday afternoon. I said I would do it, but my spirit was feeling that this was inconsiderate because I had driven more than four hundred miles the previous day. This would be another one hundred sixty miles. Couldn't somebody else have done this? When we got to camp, I helped the boy with his bags and then began walking around the camp.

Then, something happened. As I walked about the camp, I heard the noise of young children. Suddenly, the dark cloud over my spirit lifted. For the first time in months, I felt alive. I felt joy.

I got back into the car and headed back to Cochrane. As I traveled, I knew I was going back to school. I was going to go to Waterloo University College. I was then going to become a teacher at Banting Memorial High School in Alliston, where I had spent six years. And all of this actually happened in the next three years.

At the camp, I discovered that young people are my life blood. There was a highway ahead for me; the mountain disappeared. God, through His Holy Spirit, had chosen that moment to reveal what He had been gradually showing me during previous months.

CHAPTER 9

THE UNIVERSITY YEARS

Do your best to present yourself to God as one approved, a workman who does not need to be ashamed and who correctly handles the word of truth.

—2 TIMOTHY 2:15

The year with the six-point charge turned into three months. Even at that, it was a long three months, as I prepared to go to school. At the same time, it was a valuable time because I was shown that a pastoral ministry was not for me. Since I was not going to be a full-time minister, I agreed with God that I would give any money I received from the ministry to His work. That meant I would absorb the travel expenses to the speaking engagement.

I never became a typical university student. I did not want to go to school. I wanted to teach, but to do this, I had to go to school. My weekly schedule for the next three years was consistent. I would return to Waterloo on Sunday evenings and work diligently at my school work from Monday morning until Friday afternoon. Then I would leave my books at the school and not look at them again until Monday morning.

I felt a need to be successful at school for my parents' sake. They had always stood by me. They were supportive when it took two years to pass my senior year, when I did not go back to Bob Jones University and when I went as a lay supply preacher. And after a few questions about why I was going to school in Waterloo, my dad joined my mother in supporting my decision.

We were not a wealthy family. My dad and mom had worked hard and had always been able to provide our family with the essentials. I had no money because any funds I had were spent on the new Volkswagen. I had earned sufficient money from my summer pastoral job to pay my tuition and buy books and clothes.

Dad said he and Mother would give me $25 every two weeks. My room cost $13 every two weeks, leaving $12 for food and other expenses. On Sunday nights, Mom would pack me several sandwiches and cookies, which I took back to school. I would eat the sandwiches for lunch and dinner with soup and milk on Monday, Tuesday and Wednesday. I would buy two pieces of toast, milk and two pieces of bacon for my breakfast.

I began giving a ride to a couple of boys from our area who also were enrolled at Waterloo. In turn, they gave me money for gas. Sometimes I even had a dollar or two left over.

Waterloo University College was sponsored by a branch of the Lutheran church. There was a time set aside for chapel, but it was not compulsory. I always went. Although the music was not my style, it was always good to praise God. The speakers would talk for about fifteen minutes. The one presentation I remember was by a man who said the success of a person could be measured by the way he or she read the newspaper. If a person began at the front of the paper and gradually read through it, he or she would be a success. I knew immediately that I would not be, as I had always begun with the comics, then moved to the sports page, and then read the rest of the paper if time permitted.

In my second and third years at the university, I joined the committee that was in charge of the chapel and became involved with the Inter-School Christian Fellowship Program. I was its president my final year at school. The group decided to do something off campus. There was one mission for the poor in the area, and a group of us decided to go each Monday to speak and to help serve dinner. I often went.

I became friends with one of the men who seemed to always be there for the service and the meal. One Monday night, he asked me to eat at his table. It was not our group's practice to eat while at the mission, so I declined the invitation. His friendship with me died at that moment. After that happened, I reminded myself that Jesus washed the feet of His disciples.

The university was holding its first winter carnival, which included a snow sculpture contest. The

Inter-School Christian Fellowship decided to make a sculpture. We reproduced the school crest in ice, and one of the boys developed a moving cross in the middle of the crest. Our group won first prize.

In my second year, I decided to go out for the school hockey team. I was a great skater but had played most of my hockey in the goal. I could skate as fast as anyone on the team, and I felt I had an excellent chance of making the team. The last practice before the first exhibition game was on a Sunday morning. I had already promised my roommate, Alex Taylor, that I would speak at a youth service in his church that day. I would not change this commitment. I told the coach that I would not be there for practice, and he was not happy.

I went to Holstein and spoke, and the minister of the church gave me $15. I remember heading back to college thinking that $15 was more than all the money in my pockets. The $15 went to "Back to the Bible" with Theodore Epp before it had a chance to rest in my pocket.

When I went to the arena to see the list of players for the Monday night hockey game, my name was not on the list. On Tuesday morning, my Spanish teacher returned a test that I had failed. I never went back to hockey. I could not let my dad and mom down. I would not fail. Besides, if I played hockey at the school, I could not go home to Beeton on the weekends.

CHAPTER 10

THE WEEKENDS

In the same way, faith by itself, if it is not accompanied by action, is dead.

—JAMES 2:17

Weekends—this is where real life was! On Saturday morning, I would be at the arena from 8 A.M. to 1 P.M. in charge of all the house league hockey for children under twelve. This was volunteer work. I continued to coach the Peewee and Atom teams that I had begun two years before. I would have the opportunity of coaching three Little NHL Ontario championship teams.

A boy who played on one of these teams, Wayne Carleton, played in the NHL and the World Hockey

Association for more than ten years. Another player, Jim Rutherford, would play in the NHL for fourteen years. Jim played in Pittsburgh and Detroit with stopovers in Toronto and Los Angeles. Now he is president of the Carolina Hurricanes. A third player, John Gould, would play in the NHL with Vancouver, Atlanta and Buffalo for almost ten years. John's brother Larry would play pro hockey for more than fourteen years, including a handful of games in the NHL. Paul Sinclair would play Junior A hockey. John Boyce would play college hockey in Boston and would be named an American Athlete of the Year. Gene and Mike Archambeaut would receive scholarships to play in the U.S. college league. Raymond Lisk would be an MVP at Western University in the Canadian University League.

On Sunday mornings, I taught the younger youth class. One of the girls, Sylvia Lisk, has become an outstanding leader in the Catholic church. She was one of the young workers in the Catholic charismatic movement in the early 1970s. Rilla Watson has become the backbone of much of the ladies' work at Beeton Church.

During this time, Jean McKelvie Platt was working in the Sunday school as I did. We were the same age. Forty years later, she is the choir leader in the church.

Within a year, I once again became the Sunday school superintendent. On one occasion, I came home during the week to attend a meeting at Reverend Jim Shilton's church in Alliston. The new curriculum of the United Church was coming out, and I was opposed to the liberal slant. Rev. Shilton was always a strong supporter of the church in which he was ordained.

Within ten years from the beginning of the teaching of the new curriculum, many of the Sunday schools within the United Church were dead or dying. Many of the evangelicals of the church had left. This included a number of the best Sunday school teachers. There were others of us who were led to stay and work within the church. This gave me an opportunity to be a missionary within the confines of my own church.

At the conclusion of my first year at school, I was invited to speak at the United Church in Cookstown. During the next twenty-four years, I had the opportunity of speaking in this church at least twice a year. Some years, I had the opportunity to speak five or six times. The money for speaking in Cookstown was always given back to the church.

I remember speaking in Trinity United in Beeton on one Sunday and then speaking at St. Andrews Presbyterian in Beeton the next Sunday. The same message was preached to all, regardless of the church. The package may be adjusted, but the message must be the same.

I was able to organize a small band of musicians from our community that sometimes provided music for the services at the church in Beeton. I played the clarinet.

Also, with the help of a man named Metz Hill, I was able to organize a Peewee and an Atom baseball team. Many of the boys who played hockey also played baseball. In later years, those boys brought seven Ontario championships to the village.

I cannot forget the most important person in my life. I met Cathy at a Teen Town dance when I came home from my first week at the university. I was the big-shot freshman wearing my college beanie hat. I was also the "big" former two-year president of the high school Student Council. I danced with Cathy Williams that night, but I was disappointed when another girl wore my cap home.

The next week, I returned to Teen Town, where a mutual friend told me there was a girl who would like to dance with me. I replied, "Let me describe her." I gave the description, and as I hoped, it was Cathy. It would be wrong to call it love at first sight, but it certainly was a mutual fascination, which, six years later, would lead to marriage. I was a college freshman, and Cathy was a fifteen-year-old who had just entered her junior year in high school. This young lady had a lot of growing up to do. The Lord realized that I, too, had many areas in which to grow before marriage.

Two factors were important to the growth of our relationship. Cathy was a member of the United Church who had attended the Inter-Varsity Christian Fellowship Pioneer Camp, where she had accepted Jesus. Her attendance at worship on Sunday was regular, especially for a member of the United Church, where many people seem to believe that God goes on holidays in the summer. I had known Cathy's mother for years. She was the regular supply teacher at the high school. She had been in charge of my class on numerous occasions. I was immediately impressed. If Cathy was Mrs. Williams' daughter, she must be a great girl, I thought. The fact that Mrs. Williams knew who I was probably helped her to give her sixteen-year-old daughter permission to go out with this twenty-one-year-old university student.

CHAPTER 11

TO GOD BE THE GLORY

You shall not make for yourself an idol in the form of anything in heaven above or on the earth beneath or in the waters below. You shall not bow down to them or worship them; for I, the LORD your God, am a jealous God, punishing the children for the sin of the fathers to the third and fourth generation of those who hate me, but showing love to a thousand generations of those who love me and keep my commandments.

EXODUS 20:4–6

The first verse of Psalm 112 reads, "Praise ye the LORD. Blessed is the man that feareth the LORD, that delighteth greatly in his commandments" (KJV).

This verse is good for at least ten thousand sermons. For me, it means that I should love and honor my heavenly Father. As a result, I have tried, with the help of His

Holy Spirit, to show respect and love in many ways.

After fifty years as a student and a teacher, I can say that I never did any school work on Sunday. This might require me to get up at 3 A.M. on a Monday to study for a test or exam that day. Sunday is His day. As I reflect on this and other ways that I have tried to show respect, keep in mind that it is of no credit to me. It is to His glory. I have never shopped on Sunday. Sometimes we have forgotten to get bread, butter or something else that we needed, and I have gone to the store on occasion to pick it up. This chapter describes many inconsistent behaviors in my actions.

The most important thing to do on Sunday is worship God. This is essential. This does not require a formal church service, but in most cases, it requires a worship time with other members of God's family. The checks for the offering are dated Saturday or Monday. Personal banking can be handled in six days.

God says that the tithe belongs to Him. As best as I can recall, I have always given God His tithe. Any money that I have received from being a lay minister for forty-six years has nothing to do with the tithe. The money from lay preaching belongs to God. This is an agreement between this child of God and his heavenly Father. The tithe is separate.

I usually have avoided playing cards on Sunday. Since it is not one of my favorite pastimes, this has not been difficult. There have been times that I have read or talked with others while a game of cards takes place in the same room. I try not to go to a movie theater on Sunday, although the TV is allowed to play in our house.

Swear words have never been part of my vocabulary.

Interestingly enough, I often used the word "bloody" until I became aware of the deep sacredness of Christ's blood. I was well into my adult years before this happened.

I have refused to call my minister anything except reverend or pastor. My elders and bosses are Mr. and Mrs. I agree that respect depends on one's attitude rather than titles. But for me, I must show proper respect to these people as I attempt to do for my heavenly Father. Without hesitation, men's hats are not to be worn in any house—and certainly not in the house of God. This is respect toward people whose homes we enter, toward women and toward my heavenly Father.

The development of Sunday as a day for sports over the past fifty years has caused me much distress. Having coached more than two hundred teams in various sports, I have tried to keep Sunday as free from sports as possible. But it hasn't always been easy. If a Sunday game was unavoidable, it would never be scheduled during normal "church hours." Sometimes that meant games would be played 7:30 A.M.! What else could I do? Coaching has been one way that God has taken my life to be used as an influence for Him. When we are requested to play early on a Sunday, we have a chapel service. For the past twenty-five years, we have prayed before every game, regardless of the day.

Grace is said before most meals, regardless of where we are.

This chapter has nothing to do with a suggested method of behavior for anyone else. This chapter is about my relationship with my heavenly Father.

CHAPTER 12

YOUNG PEOPLE ARE MY LIFE BLOOD

Jesus came and told his disciples, "I have been given complete authority in heaven and on earth. Therefore, go and make disciples of all the nations, baptizing them in the name of the Father and the Son and the Holy Spirit. Teach these new disciples to obey all the commands I have given you. And be sure of this: I am with you always, even to the end of the age."
—MATTHEW 28:18–20, NLT

S ince it was revealed to me on that road from Timmins to Cochrane that young people are my life blood, I have never faltered from that path.

After teaching all day, I often have been in the arena, at the ballpark, at the track, in the gymnasium or on the soccer field working as a volunteer with various sports teams as soon as the school day was over. I have been known to complete a school year and leave within a week for a thousand-mile tour with fifteen ball players in my van. The tour could last as long as three weeks. I might be the only adult traveling with the players, who could be an Atom team of eight- and nine-year-olds or a Bantam team of thirteen- and fourteen-year-olds. It could be fifteen girl basketball players heading for the National Fellowship of Christian Athletes Camp in Marshall, Indiana. It might be a trip to Barrie sixty miles away for a one-day tournament.

There were lessons to learn, and there still are.

During my second year at school, I was coaching our Peewee hockey team in the Ontario championship. My mother knew all of our game times. I knew she would be praying for the team. This tournament was to declare the rural Ontario champion with the winner going to the Ontario Open Championship in three weeks. My final exams were scheduled to begin in three weeks and two days. I did not tell my mother that if we won, we would be playing on the weekend prior to these exams. I was afraid that if I told her, she would not be inspired to pray for my team. We reached the Ontario rural finals. In our semifinal game, our team had played to its full potential and beat the team that I considered our main rival.

We would play Burk's Falls from Northern Ontario in the finals. The win was as good as in our pocket. After two periods, we were ahead 3-1 and had control of the game. Early in the third period, Jimmy Rutherford, our goalie, got cut over his eye. Goalie masks had yet to be invented. His mom, dad and I agreed that Jimmy with one eye was better than our other goalie with two eyes.

Our team had three penalties called against us in the

next few minutes. Although none of the calls were for flagrant violations, the calls were valid. Burk's Falls scored each time. We lost the game and the championship 4 to 3.

I went home and told Mother about my exam schedule and why I had not told her. Mother never blinked an eye and said, "Ronald, I did not know your exam schedule, but God did."

I passed my school year. The hockey team won the championship the next season.

CHAPTER 13

WAYNE

For since in the wisdom of God the world through its wisdom did not know him, God was pleased through the foolishness of what was preached to save those who believe. Jews demand miraculous signs and Greeks look for wisdom, but we preach Christ crucified: a stumbling block to Jews and foolishness to Gentiles, but to those whom God has called, both Jews and Greeks, Christ the power of God and the wisdom of God. For the foolishness of God is wiser than man's wisdom, and the weakness of God is stronger than man's strength.

—1 CORINTHIANS 1:21–25

Wayne was in my first home-form class in my first year of teaching. He chose to sit in the front seat on the right side of the room. It was the closest seat to the door. Wayne was a great attention-seeker. He was inclined to be a nuisance in the room and was not much of a student.

At the end of the first month of school, the teachers of all the freshmen met with the school administration to decide which students from this group should be placed in special education for slow learners. I was one of the teachers who suggested Wayne for this class. He was chosen. It made life more pleasant in my home-form class. When I would see Wayne in the hall, I would speak to him. I would hear periodically about him being in trouble. I was never surprised.

It was during my first year of teaching in this school that the principal had asked me to form an Inter-School Christian Fellowship group. On one occasion two years later, as I arrived for an Inter-School meeting, I could not believe who I saw walking through the door. It was Wayne! We exchanged greetings, and he took a seat. In my "great faith," I thought Wayne must have made a mistake—he probably thought this room was the detention room. Other kids came to the room, and Wayne stayed. The meeting began, and Wayne still stayed. He became a regular member of the group.

The next year, Wayne was a member of my advanced junior history class. His final grade was almost an A. At the end of the school year, promotion meetings were held, and Wayne had passed his year with a B+ average.

After Wayne was discussed at the meeting, one of the teachers asked, "Isn't this one of the kids that we put in the slow learners class? What happened to him?" Another teacher replied, "Jesus Christ happened to him." Wayne graduated from high school and became a minister.

What had happened? Wayne and three of his friends had decided to enter the local barbershop after it was closed. They entered through the basement. They planned to steal the barber's money but could not find it. The group decided to come back the next night. The barber would leave some this time, they thought. Again, there was no money. They decided to try it a third night in a row. The barber and a police officer were waiting.

One of the results of Wayne's trial conviction was that he was required to go to church each Sunday. Wayne chose to attend the nearby First Assembly Church. He listened to a number of altar calls. One Sunday, Wayne got up during an alter call, but he did not head to the altar. Instead he quickly left the church. He hitchhiked around the surrounding area for the entire afternoon. In the early evening, he found himself on the Cookstown road heading toward his home. On that road, Wayne gave up running and accepted Christ.

When Wayne was in his last year of high school, I went to teach at another school. I was invited back to speak to the Inter-School Christian Fellowship group. After the meeting was over, Wayne came to me, and we shook hands and talked for a couple of minutes. Then Wayne asked me if I had ever received the baptism of the Holy Spirit. I said the Holy Spirit came and lived within me when I accepted Jesus. Wayne insisted, "But have you received the baptism of the Holy Spirit?" After a few minutes of disagreeing, I thanked Wayne and left.

For the first time in my Christian life, at twenty-seven years of age, I had been openly confronted about the baptism of God's Holy Spirit. Because God had spoken to me through Wayne, I certainly thought about what he had said. I thought about it much more than if any minister had spoken to me on the same subject.

CHAPTER 14

STAN IZON

When I came to you, brothers, I did not come with eloquence or superior wisdom as I proclaimed to you the testimony about God. For I resolved to know nothing while I was with you except Jesus and him crucified.

—1 CORINTHIANS 2:1–2

S tan Izon, who came from Toronto, worked with the youth in his Anglican (Church of England) diocese. Along with the youth, he often went out for youth outreach meetings.

Doug Nesbitt, a teacher of mine with whom I was then teaching at Banting in Alliston, went to the Anglican church. He was aware of Stan's work. During my second year of teaching, Doug suggested that on the following Saturday night, some of the youth and I go to Markdale, an hour's drive, to hear Stan Izon. A couple of carloads went with Doug and me.

Stan was not an emotional speaker, although he was sound. One of his favorite phrases was, "Trust and obey, or you will rust and decay." At the close of the service, many of the youth in the church went forward to accept Christ.

Doug and I talked about having Stan come to Alliston. Ken Inkster, an organist and choir director who was also head of the school's language department, joined our discussions.

Ken had introduced me to a prayer group in Alliston that met on Wednesday at Mrs. Murphy's home. We mentioned bringing Stan to Alliston. The prayer group was enthusiastic. A group of women at my home church in Beeton, led by Hazel McCague and Helen Dale, was also enthusiastic.

There was a large number of youth around to help develop this meeting. The Inter-School Christian Fellowship group at the high school had more than twenty members. My teenage Sunday school classes had a regular attendance of fifteen. The youth group in the Cookstown United Church, where I had been ministering in the summer for the past six years, was very active.

Mr. Inkster asked Reverend Jim Shilton to host the meeting in his church. Rev. Shilton agreed.

On a Friday evening, St. John's United Church in Alliston was full of young people to hear the gospel. A number of them responded to the altar call. After the meeting, it was decided to invite Stan and his youth back in a few months for a day of teaching with the local youth. An evening service would close out the day.

Where would we hold this meeting? Rev. Shilton was not pleased with the strong evangelical thrust of our meeting at his church. He did not wish to host another meeting. Trinity United in Beeton, my home church, would be the host.

Our prayer group in Alliston doubled its efforts. The women's group in the Beeton area increased its prayer focus toward the youth. I began working with a youth committee, which had developed from the first meeting.

Many of the young people had never prayed in a group meeting. Some of them began to pray after we had met a number of times. The Saturday arrived, and more than forty of our youth took part in the day of discipleship. Almost one hundred youth sat down for the dinner that the women of our church had prepared.

The church auditorium was packed with young people. When Stan Izon gave the altar call, most of the seats became empty. The altar was full.

Stan had a monthly newsletter. Our meetings in Beeton dominated the next issue. Stan felt that the format we had followed should become an example for similar meetings that he would hold in the future.

One of the key to the meetings' success was that they had been preceded with much prayer. Another key was the "sowing of seeds" by many people during the previous three years.

CHAPTER 15

CHRISTIANITY IS 24 HOURS A DAY, 7 DAYS A WEEK

Let us not become weary in doing good, for at the proper time we will reap a harvest if we do not give up.

—GALATIANS 6:9

Jesus never goes on vacation. His phone lines are always open. He is always available.

It is not easy to even begin to approach the standards of Jesus. However, with His help and control, a person can begin to approach those standards. As Anita Bryant has written in one of her songs, "I am what I am by the grace of my God."

In my last year at school, I applied to the Ontario government for a "needs bursary." I received $200 in

January. For me, this was a lot of money. What would I do with all of this money? I had many wonderful ideas.

A month later, when I was returning to school on Sunday evening, I heard a loud "clunk" as I turned a corner. The transmission had gone out of my Volkswagen. The bill came to $192.50. The Lord had provided for my need even before I knew I had it.

When I finished school, I had no debt.

Another time, early in March of my final year at school, I was at the mission in Waterloo. As we were being led in prayer, God said to me, "Cathy is the girl for you." That was great news! (By the way, one of the ideas I had for the $200 bursary was to buy Cathy, who was in her last year of high school, an engagement ring.) This was a Monday night. On Friday evening of that same week, Cathy and I went to a dance at her school. When I took her home that evening, she said she no longer wanted to go steady. I had no choice but to agree.

I went home. That night I could not sleep. Had God not told me that she was the girl for me? The next morning, I went to the arena for hockey. It was a long morning. Hockey was not on my mind.

Cathy and I would go out on a date now and then, and she was very cool toward me. But in spite of this, I invited her to my graduation party in May. She eventually agreed to come, but she was not pleasant company.

I continued to talk to God about this situation. Had I misunderstood Him? After the graduation weekend, I told God that I needed an answer in six months. I didn't think I could stand being in this situation any longer than that.

As time went by, our dates became further and further

apart. By the first of September, we were not even speaking.

In late September, she was leaving to go to college. I was teaching in the high school. Her brother was playing football on the team I was coaching. Cathy came to pick him up after practice. She invited me to come to her home that evening. She needed some books for school, and maybe I had some of them.

I went, and we had a great evening. She agreed to go to her fall graduation with me, even though this meant that she had to cancel a date with another guy.

In mid-November, a friend of Cathy's went to visit her at school. The next Friday night, I was staff supervisor of a dance at the high school. Cathy's friend came and told me that Cathy had told her the previous weekend that I was the guy for her. It was six months to the day since I had talked with my heavenly Father about needing an answer in six months. It had been a tough six months for me. I can only assume that this is the reason that He had spoken to me at the mission. Without His words, I don't know what might have happened.

In my second year of teaching, I began to visit Cathy at her school on weekends. We always went to church. One Sunday morning, we were in the church of a former moderator (head of the church for two years) of the United Church. During his sermon, he said, "There are no fundamentalist, Bible-thumping people in this church. I got rid of them a long time ago." I wanted to stand up and say, "I am here, and I fit your description."

God has never provided me with a comfortable pew, but He has always been there for me in His time and in His way.

Cathy was a member of Reverend Jim Shilton's church. He was their family minister for many years. He eventually would perform our wedding ceremony in 1965, and he would later dedicate all three of our children. This included coming to our church in Flesherton in 1979 to dedicate Stacey. Prior to the Stacey's dedication, he had been sick, and it was the first public event he had participated in since his illness.

Cathy and I worshiped in his church in Alliston for much of the first six years of our marriage. During that time, we went to her parents' home on weekends and spent much of our summers at their farm.

I often disagreed with Rev. Shilton's theological slant. But eventually, I stopped confronting him, and we no longer discussed our theological differences. There was no question of his love for the people he served at that church for more than twenty-five years. There was no question that he was a fine man who was dedicated to the work of his Lord and Savior. As I matured, I came to appreciate his servitude. We had become good friends, and we held a mutual respect for each other.

CHAPTER 16

A COMMUNITY UPSET

My God, my God, why have you forsaken me?...I cry out...but you do not answer.

—PSALM 22:1–2

I t was a Monday morning in August in the early '60s. I had finished summer school a week before and was sleeping in. Before 8:30 A.M., Mother came upstairs to my room. This meant something important was happening.

Thomasina Baker was missing. She had disappeared from her parents' home next door the previous evening. A number of people had been out searching for the twelve-year-old all night.

The Bakers were close to me. I had been best man at

Thomasina's brother's wedding. Her sister was in the same youth group as I. Thomasina and her mother had been in church in Beeton that Sunday morning when I was preaching.

I was soon helping with the search. In the evening, I was in the barn with the Bakers as they attempted to carry on a semblance of normal life. I went to the house and spent a couple of hours with Mr. and Mrs. Baker. We prayed together. I did not go home that night. I stayed in their yard along with the police. I fell asleep just before the sun came up.

By Tuesday, there were more than three hundred people searching for the girl. I walked the search areas side by side with her brother, Albert. Tuesday ended with no more clues than when it started.

I took Mr. and Mrs. Baker to the church that evening for prayer. Our minister was on vacation. After bringing the Bakers back to the farm, I went home to sleep.

Wednesday brought no new clues, either. The Bakers and I once again went to the church.

Thursday was interesting. Police asked more than forty people from our village who worked in a sporting goods factory in Toronto to stay home from work on Thursday. The police needed these people, who were familiar with the area, to lead search groups. By now, the number of searchers was approaching eight hundred.

The head of the factory called the employees to a meeting Wednesday afternoon. He told them that he expected them to be at work on Thursday; if they were not, they would lose their jobs.

On Thursday morning, all of these people joined the search. When they returned to work on Friday, they still had their jobs. But unfortunately, Thursday brought no answers. Again, I took Mr. and Mrs. Baker to the church Thursday night.

The next day, plans were under way for a massive weekend search. The search headquarters moved from the Baker farm to the local arena. More than five thousand people would join the search on Saturday.

Our minister arrived home Friday and took over going with the Bakers to the church.

Neither Saturday's nor Sunday's massive search turned up any clues. The public search ended Sunday, but a team of detectives continued to search for clues.

A year went by. We heard nothing. Her body finally was discovered in a grave less than fifteen miles from her home two days before President Kennedy was assassinated.

A memorial service was held in our church the day after the assassination. I had sometimes sung duets in the church, and Mrs. Baker asked me to sing "When He Cometh to Take Home His Jewels."

The Bakers were never the same. Eventually, they sold their farm and moved. Our community was also never the same.

And I would never be the same. How could I? I had lived a week with the Bakers during their terrible anguish. I saw the toll that the ordeal had taken on the family—the agony of not knowing where their sweet Thomasina was. I had also suffered much personal anguish. I knew that the only comfort that the Bakers received had come from the Lord Jesus. They did not blame God. They did not question God. They relied on the one and only great Comforter.

CHAPTER 17

LIFE BEYOND BANTING

The apostles and the brothers throughout Judea heard that the Gentiles also had received the word of God.

—Acts 11:1

I have heard it said that if you want to hear God laugh, tell Him about your plans.

Since God showed me that young people were my life blood, I had taken for granted that I would teach my entire career at Banting. He had shown me that I was going to Banting. There were a half-dozen teachers whom I admired who had spent their career in Banting. I expected to follow in their footsteps. How little I knew.

Cathy and I were engaged to be married in June, 1965. I had completed four years of teaching at Banting. She had completed one year of teaching at Huron Heights in Newmarket, where she was head of the girls' physical education program. In my fourth year at Banting, I was acting head of history.

Huron Heights offered me the headship of history. The head at Banting was coming back. There was not a job opening in physical education at Banting. So I went to Newmarket for what ended up being six years.

In the fifth year, our first child, James David, was born. My mother-in-law's maiden name was James. Cathy's favorite uncle was also named James. David, my brother's name, had been in the Pegg family for generations. Besides, James was the brother of Jesus, and David was a forefather of Jesus.

When Cathy was pregnant with Jamie, I received one of the best pieces of advice that I have ever received. My mother said, "The time to start praying for your child is now. Don't wait until the child arrives. Begin praying now." From that day on, I followed that advice. After the children were born, I usually went to their beds each night and prayed for them. I did this until they became adults. In fact, even now on occasion, I will enter one of their rooms to pray. If I have done one thing right in life, it is this.

After Jamie was born, I learned an important lesson. Cathy was on a leave of absence from the school. I had assumed that she would not return to teaching, although we had not discussed this. My mother had always been at home with our family, and her mother, who was a high school principal in 1940, had quit her job to be with her children.

During the leave of absence, I told Cathy's replacement that she would not be coming back. I told my wife that evening, and she broke into tears. The next day, I informed Cathy's replacement that I had spoken out of turn. Cathy planned to return. Never again would I make a plan for my wife without her input.

The minister of the United Church in Newmarket had said from the pulpit that he wasn't sure that Christ had risen from the dead. In spite of this, I volunteered twice to teach Sunday school. I never got a response. However, we were often in Alliston on the weekends, so Cathy's church became our main place of worship.

On Sundays, when we were in Newmarket, Cathy often chose to let me go to church by myself. I visited many of the area's churches. I began to work with the local ministerial fellowship in the town, especially through the Inter-School Christian Fellowship Group that I had started at the school.

We ran a series of coffee houses in the Presbyterian church on Friday nights. Various Christian music groups were invited to lead. We also worked with a local Baptist church to hold an outreach weekend. During one summer, we ran a coffee house seven nights a week in an empty commercial building in downtown Newmarket.

Meanwhile, I had applied for director of sports in the secondary schools of Ontario. I was one of three finalists but did not get the job.

My good friend Norm Menczel and I had asked for the right to hold an invitational soccer tournament to see if there was enough interest for soccer to become an official sport of the schools. We had twenty-two schools the first year. This one-day tournament grew rapidly to one hundred twenty teams at its largest point. Soccer became an official sport of high schools, and I became its first provincial convener.

During this time, Mrs. Aldom, one of three secretaries at the school, often invited me to speak to her church's youth. The church she attended was in the country outside of Newmarket.

I often felt that I was not really baptized since my only experience with baptism had been the sprinkling at my dedication in the United Church in Beeton. I began to feel a need to experience the believer's baptism. I was baptized on a Sunday evening while church organist Keith Profit played my then favorite gospel song, "He Touched Me." After the baptism, I felt a new freedom and a closer relationship with Jesus.

Back at school, I applied for the high school principal's course, even though I was not recommended for it. When I began teaching, my desire was to become a principal.

When I was being interviewed by the superintendent for the job, I said, "Until God wants me to be a principal, no man will make me a principal. And when God wants me to be a principal, no man will stop me from becoming one."

It was never God's wish for me to become a principal. It took me another fifteen years to realize it. But then, I understood why.

In the meantime, I had begun to work on my master's degree in education in planning at the University of Toronto as a part-time and summer student.

CHAPTER 18

A SUCCESSFUL COFFEE HOUSE

About midnight Paul and Silas were praying and singing hymns to God, and the other prisoners were listening to them. Suddenly there was such a violent earthquake that the foundations of the prison were shaken. At once all the prison doors flew open, and everybody's chains came loose. The jailer woke up, and when he saw the prison doors open, he drew his sword and was about to kill himself because he thought the prisoners had escaped. But Paul shouted, "Don't harm yourself! We are all here!" The jailer called for lights, rushed in and fell trembling before Paul and Silas. He then brought them out and asked, "Sirs, what must I do to be saved?" They answered, "Believe in the Lord Jesus, and you will be saved—you and your household."
—ACTS 16:25–31

Pastor Hepner of Grace Church in Newmarket was concerned with the youth. While in Newmarket, I probably worked more closely with him than with any other minister.

He had made arrangements for a Youth for Christ ministry team to come to town and have a one-week series of coffee house meetings in downtown Newmarket. He asked if I could arrange a school assembly through Inter-School Christian Fellowship. Our principal agreed.

The week before the scheduled assembly, I received word that our principal was not so sure that it should take place. I needed to talk to the principal about the future of the assembly. I felt the assembly was an important part of the future success of the coffee house outreach. So, a meeting was arranged.

I called my mother. She had been my main prayer support. I asked her to pray for my meeting with the principal. I also spoke to Mrs. Aldom in the office to make sure she was praying. I paced the floors of the school for more than half an hour. I was seeking God's guidance and peace.

It was time for the meeting. After we talked for more than twenty minutes, the principal agreed to hold the assembly. It was scheduled for Monday morning with the coffee house meeting beginning that evening. Forty-seven students from our school accepted Christ that week at the coffee house.

It has been interesting to watch God use Inter-School in my life. We had a great group when I was in Alliston, but it never seemed to get off the ground at Huron

Heights, except that it was the vehicle for the assembly. Most Inter-School Christian Fellowship meetings had six or seven young people in attendance. Those who went were from good Christian homes.

For a number of years, a group of teachers met for prayer at least once a week. We prayed for the youth. Why wasn't the Inter-School group growing?

Peggy Aldon, our secretary's daughter, always attended the meetings. Her brother, David, had come on staff. He was one of the people who made up our prayer fellowship. A year after Peggy graduated from school, I got a letter from her.

She thanked me for the Inter-School Christian Fellowship. She said the group meetings had been important to her accepting Christ as her Savior a few months earlier. I was shocked that she had just accepted Christ. I had assumed she was a Christian all the time she was in the group.

During the next couple of years, I received other letters and was involved in conversations that revealed that most of the small groups had come to Christ only after they left high school and home.

How could these young people reach out when they had nothing to reach out with?

CHAPTER 19

RESTLESSNESS

The following night the Lord stood near Paul and said, "Take courage! As you have testified about me in Jerusalem, so must you also testify in Rome."
—ACTS 23:11

Newmarket had been good to us. My wife and I had made many good friends. I could not have asked for a better group of people with whom to work in the history department. The people in physical health education were just as great. Other staff members were always cooperative.

I had begun to coach girls' basketball teams at the school. I had teams go from the district to the regional championships each year. I had begun a school variety show. I even wrote much of the script. The auditorium would be full for two nights to see this show. The dress rehearsal was held with an invited audience of senior citizens from various retirement homes in the Newmarket area.

I was coaching a boys' baseball team of nine and ten-year-olds. I had begun a league called York Simcoe so Newmarket would have a league.

Our son Jamie was a healthy one-year-old. We had a woman come to our house each day to look after him.

But I was restless. For almost a year, I continually would seek for God to show me what I should be doing and where I should be. No answer came. The more time that went by, the more restless I became.

It seemed out of nowhere that an ad appeared in the paper for a job in Flesherton. It was a small, rural community almost the size of Beeton, where I had spent my childhood. I spoke with Cathy about it. There were no jobs advertised for her. She said I could call for an interview. I was to go the next day.

There were one hundred fifty job applicants, but the vice principal of the Flesherton school had been speaking with Mike Steele, the vice principal in Newmarket, and the job was mine if I wanted it. But I wondered, *Was this what I was supposed to be doing?* I asked for forty-eight hours to decide. Cathy and I discussed it with her mother and with my dad and mom. I discussed it with my history department. There were prayers to God.

After forty-eight hours, I called the principal, Mr. Juffs, and asked for another forty-eight hours. I already knew in my heart that I had to go, but Cathy was not prepared to give an answer.

Going to Flesherton meant giving up my department headship. I would be a teacher in a small department. Cathy would not even have a job, but she would be able to get a lot of supply work.

I thought of Beeton. I was not a great athlete. I was just a boy who loved to play. I always had a good time because there were just enough kids in Beeton to form a ball team or a hockey team. Every kid got a chance to play. It was not this way in Newmarket. I wanted Jamie to have an opportunity to have fun in sports. Flesherton probably could provide this. We saw the new arena that was scheduled to be completed in the fall.

When I saw Flesherton, I saw a dream that I had always had. I thought the dream was to return to Beeton, but Flesherton appeared to be the place of my dreams. I felt I had to go.

It came down to the last hour before I was to call. Cathy still had not given me an answer. I had to go on a family errand. I told Cathy I had to call Mr. Juffs when I returned. As I drove, I asked God, "What do I do if Cathy says no? What do I do?"

When I returned home, I told Cathy I was calling. I asked her what I should say. She replied that it was up to me. I said that I would be accepting the position. As I talked to Mr. Juffs with absolute joy in my heart, tears were streaming down my wife's face as she sat at the kitchen table.

CHAPTER 20

FLESHERTON

For he looked for a city which hath foundations,
whose builder and maker is God.
                                        —*HEBREWS 11:10 KJV*

It was fall 1971. We had moved to Flesherton. My restlessness had gone away. I was full of excitement, even though my wife did not share the same level of enthusiastic anticipation.

I felt at home as soon as I arrived. The Lord had revealed to me that there would be a hockey dynasty and a girls' basketball dynasty. This would be to His glory.

St. John's United Church was a friendly, small-town church. Mr. Juffs asked me to begin an Inter-School

Christian Fellowship at the school. I became the coach of the senior girls' basketball team. I participated in a walk-a-thon to help raise money for the arena. I was going to be one of the coaches of the Atom hockey team.

We had a beautiful new home. Mrs. Robinson, the doctor's wife, was interested in education as part of her concern for the community. She had a vision to help new teachers come to the village. There were not many new homes in the village. She had two houses built to encourage teachers to live in the community. We lived in one of them.

The girls' basketball season was a great success. The team advanced to the regional championships when Susan Pattison scored at the end of overtime. Grey Highlands of Flesherton had not had a team go to CWOSSA in its previous four years.

When the natural ice was finally in the arena just after Christmas, I held my first hockey practice. When I asked the boys to skate backward around the ice, I didn't think that these nine and ten-year-olds would ever get around the ice. We played an exhibition game in Beeton. The final score was 10-0, Beeton. Our first star was our goaltender. It was quite a start for a dynasty, but the Flesherton kids had not had an arena for more than five years.

My wife was soon teaching on a contract basis.

Mrs. Robinson wanted me to become the Sunday school superintendent, but I did not feel that was where I should be at that time.

My new history boss, Gil Little, already was developing into a good friend as well as an excellent boss.

On the first day of school, Mr. Juffs introduced the head custodian at the school assembly, saying this is the man who really runs this school.

The dream was becoming a reality.

CHAPTER 21

THE EARLY YEARS

And without faith it is impossible to please God, because anyone who comes to him must believe that he exists and that he rewards those who earnestly seek him.

—Hebrews 11:6

D uring our first summer in Flesherton, Cathy and I took our young child with us to a Fellowship of Christian Athletes conference in Mount Pleasant, Michigan. This was our first exposure to this organization, one that Branch Rickey had helped to establish.

From the return to Flesherton until this day, I have always had prayer before any of my teams' games.

I discovered that the Fellowship of Christian Athletes had only one member who was a hockey player. During the coming year, I sent a letter to each player in the National Hockey League encouraging him to join FCA. Hockey needed this witness. Three players replied indicating they had some interest in getting involved.

I also wrote to the FCA office in Kansas City and pointed out that the FCA did not have an office in Canada. I said I would be happy to have my post office box in Flesherton as an FCA mail box. I would voluntarily do any of the office work that would be necessary. FCA showed no interest in this offer. The organization has never come to have a major Canadian influence.

Within a couple of years, Athletes in Action became a Canadian organization. One of its founders was Larry Kerychuk of Phoenix First Assembly. Larry was playing football with the Edmonton Eskimos. Within a couple of years, a Christian organization was beginning to work with Christian hockey players.

Both of these organizations were invited early in their history to come to Flesherton to be involved with the high school students.

The Inter-School Christian Fellowship at Grey Highlands was an instant success. There were more than forty regular participants. There were a number of great student leaders. This was the beginning of my discovery that I was not the key to the group's success. The key has always been the activity of the Holy Spirit plus the student Christian leadership. I am no more than God's facilitator.

In our second year at the school, the Inter-School Christian Fellowship group decided to go to the Catacombs, an organization of young charismatic Christians who met in an Anglican church in downtown

Toronto. It was a great evening. Some of our students accepted Christ; others rededicated their lives.

After the meeting, we invited David and Marg Hynes to come with a couple of the other Catacomb members to Flesherton for a Saturday night meeting at St. John's United. St. John's also invited the Hynes to be active in the Sunday morning service.

It was agreed that the Hynes would be guests in our home that Saturday night. While we were sitting in our living room talking about God, David asked me if I was a Christian, if I had accepted Christ as Lord and Savior. I immediately replied that I had. He then asked me if I had received the baptism of the Holy Spirit. After a moment, I said I thought I had. Then I began to think about what I had said.

Why had I replied without hesitation that I knew Jesus but that I *thought* I had received the baptism of the Holy Spirit?

David opened the Book of Acts and read to me. I had read it numerous times, but David's teaching was a new revelation to me. Before the day was over, I had received the baptism of the Holy Spirit. Wow! There was new opportunity, there was new enthusiasm, and there was new power.

I had been so busy working for the Lord that it had taken twenty years for me to hear the message about His Holy Spirit. Pastors Hall and Wayne had opened the door, but I was not ready to listen.

I had become a board member of St. John's Church. Our minister was leaving, and I was asked to serve on the committee to find a new minister. We interviewed Reverend Wally Leeman. I had been given the task of talking to people from his previous church. He sounded like a good man. At the interview, I had only one question. Did Rev. Leeman have any knowledge of the charismatic movement? He replied the he had some knowledge and was interested in gaining more. I moved the motion to hire Rev. Leeman.

Meanwhile, I had become the coach of both girls' basketball teams. Both teams finished one position away from the regional championships. Our Atom hockey team played its first league game at home against the league's toughest team. Honeywood beat us 17-0. We didn't get one shot on their net.

I had accepted an appointment to the arena board. The arena structure was set, but it was not completed inside. It was a bare skeleton, and one that was only half paid for.

CHAPTER 22

THE FOUNDATION IS FORMING

*But now they desire a better, that is, a heavenly
country. Therefore God is not ashamed to be called
their God, for He has prepared a city for them.*
—*HEBREWS 11:16, NKJV*

In the fall of 1973, our second son, Robert Michael
Williams Pegg, was born. Williams was Cathy's
maiden name. She also chose Robert Michael, and I
agreed.

During the previous year as Cathy taught, Wyn Smith,
our next-door neighbor, looked after Jamie in our
home. Wyn Smith was to become an institution in our
home. She was like a grandmother to our children.

The junior girls' basketball team won the district but
lost in the semifinals at the regional championship. Our

Atom hockey team became respectable in its competitions. The arena board was busy raising money to pay off the mortgage for the arena. Reverend Wally Leeman was proclaiming the gospel of Jesus Christ in our church. I had become the Sunday school superintendent, and the Inter-School Christian Fellowship continued to prosper.

I received invitations to speak at churches in Holstein, thirty minutes away from Flesherton. I did so many times during the next twenty years.

Cathy was becoming quite comfortable in Flesherton. When Dave and Marg Hynes returned to Flesherton the next year, Cathy received the baptism of the Holy Spirit in a service at St. John's, and she immediately received the gift of tongues. I had not spoken in tongues until a couple of weeks after I was baptized in the Holy Spirit.

CHAPTER 23

THE WORLD OF A SPORTS DYNASTY

The Lord is not slow in keeping his promise, as some understand slowness. He is patient with you, not wanting anyone to perish, but everyone to come to repentance.

—2 PETER 3:9

When the junior girls' basketball team won the district for the first time, it was the start of eleven consecutive championship years. The year after that, they also won the first of eight consecutive regional CWOSSA championships. When the junior team won its first regional championship, the senior girls won their first district championship. The next year, they won the regional championship 101-32.

Our school would go on to win a total of five double regional championships. Only one other school had ever won a double championship. No junior team had ever won the regionals more than two years in a row.

The senior girls had won seventy-nine consecutive league games.

In the late '70s, we took a van load of girls to Marshall, Indiana, two different years. Marshall is the national site of many Fellowship of Christian Athletes programs. We took the girls for basketball and to find out more about Jesus. Both happened.

I may have been the only public high school coach in Canada who had prayer before each game.

God had said there would be a dynasty. But if He had not been in charge, the dynasty never would have happened.

The hockey program continued to limp along. In the late '70s, our Peewee team was in the Ontario finals, but little else was happening.

Our oldest son had a group of friends who showed signs of being good hockey players. Jamie was as good as most of his friends. When these boys were seven and eight years old, we went to Honeywood to play in a tournament. We played Honeywood in the championship game, which we won 11-0. The dynasty had begun. This group would win six consecutive Ontario championships, but it was not the only team to win. From 1980 until 1991, Flesherton teams won nine Ontario championships, while having two teams in the Ontario finals.

There was never a league game scheduled in the Flesherton arena on a Sunday, although we hosted seven to twelve tournaments a year. Were Flesherton teams the only minor hockey teams in Ontario that honored God with prayer before each game? I do not know, but if there were others, the teams probably could be counted on one hand.

We never prayed for victory. We prayed to put the game in His hands. We prayed that we would have fun, and we prayed to give Him the glory.

Two of the girls' basketball players would be chosen to play on Ontario teams. Marilyn MacMillan Delaat prepared her daughter's team in 1998 to enter high school. Will the basketball dynasty return? Only God knows. Marilyn was one of two girls from our school to play on five regional championship teams. The other, Patti Elliott Mason, is busy raising her children, including Chad, who had numerous operations to survive his first two years of life.

Flesherton has now had two boys in recent years who have played in the Ontario top junior league. One is Chris Neil, who is still junior age but already has been drafted by the Ottawa Senators of the NHL. The other is our son Jamie. He has played five years in the top junior league but has never been drafted by an NHL team. He went to college, where he became a Canadian All Star both academically and as a defenseman. He was named the Western Canadian University Hockey Player of the Year. The same year, he was named the Western Canadian University Male Athlete of the Year. He has since played professional hockey in Norway, England and Temple, Texas.

As a small boy, he accepted Jesus as he knelt beside his bed. He has never looked back. Jamie was active at the University of Calgary in the Athletes in Action program. Tara Honey, his new bride and a fine Christian girl, joined him in 2000 in Temple.

Many Flesherton hockey players have now played just one level away from the top Junior rank. Flesherton's latest Ontario hockey championship team was crowned in the spring of 1998.

CHAPTER 24

COME, HOLY SPIRIT, WITH YOUR POWER AND MIGHT

Suddenly a sound like the blowing of a violent wind came from heaven and filled the whole house where they were sitting. They saw what seemed to be tongues of fire that separated and came to rest on each of them. All of them were filled with the Holy Spirit and began to speak in other tongues, as the Spirit enabled them.

—ACTS 2:2–4

In the fall of 1975, my mother and father both went to be with Jesus within a period of six weeks. Within another five weeks, I had major surgery to remove one of my kneecaps. It had fallen apart, and I couldn't bend it more than 70 degrees. Yet, those fall and winter months of 1975 and 1976 were some of the most exciting times of my life. During those "valley times," the Holy Spirit gave me God's peace through the gift of His Son, the Lord Jesus.

The most devastating part of my loss was my spiritual loneliness. My mother had always been the person with whom I could talk. Within the bounds of my church, there were not many born again, Spirit-filled Christians. But this void was soon filled.

Through services like the Hynes', new Christians were being born. The services were held in the United Church, but in the name of the Inter-School Christian Fellowship. At a Sunday school fellowship night, we showed a film about Christ's second coming. This film vividly illustrated the problem of those who were left behind. More people came to Christ. We began a family fellowship group, which met once a week during the summer at different people's homes. Reverend Wally Leeman and his wife, Wilma, were supportive. Our church was growing.

A women's prayer group became quite active, and a men's group also formed. Rev. Lehman divided up our entire village into streets that were assigned to different people for prayer. Every person in our village was on a prayer list.

A number of the men from our church became active in the Full Gospel Businessmen's Association. Many of the same men, along with their wives and family, became active in the United Church Renewal Fellowship.

In these two groups, we found the fellowship and freedom of worship that can only be provided by the Holy Spirit. I was beginning to become aware of how much the Holy Spirit had guided and influenced my life prior to my experiencing the baptism. I was also aware of how much greater the opportunity, the responsibility and the power were now that the baptism had occurred.

In the early chapters of this book, I spoke of God as I knew Him at that time. During those years, the Holy Spirit was definitely with me, guiding my steps, but I did not yet have an intimate relationship with Him.

At one of the Full Gospel meetings, my brother, David, rededicated his life to Jesus. It was an especially joyful event because David had become an alcoholic. I had cried many tears for him. I had seen him leave our home to drive home late at night when he should not have been driving. I would call out to God with tears streaming down my face for his safety and salvation. He had come to this meeting because I had invited him the previous night. His major reason for coming was because he heard the terminology *businessmen*. He and his wife had become heavily involved with Amway, and he saw the meeting as a networking opportunity.

As we were standing and praising God at the end of the breakfast, the Holy Spirit said to me, "Get out of his way. He is going." I just shoved my chair in, moved closer to the table and began to cry as I praised the name of Jesus. I didn't even dare look.

David went forward and has never looked back. His daughter married an Assembly of God minister. As a wedding gift, our family gave them a week at Tommy Barnett's Pastor's School in Phoenix. David's son recently became engaged to a young Spirit-filled woman. David's wife, Louise, should have many medals because she stood by him, along with her parents, during his time of wandering from the Lord.

CHAPTER 25

SURPRISE! A BASEBALL DYNASTY

Then Jesus lifted up His eyes, and seeing a great multitude coming toward Him, He said to Philip, "Where shall we buy bread, that these may eat?" But this He said to test him, for He Himself knew what He would do. Philip answered Him, "Two hundred denarii worth of bread is not sufficient for them, that every one of them may have a little." One of His disciples, Andrew, Simon Peter's brother, said to Him, "There is a lad here who has five barley loaves and two small fish, but what are they among so many?" Then Jesus said, "Make the people sit down." Now there was much grass in the place. So the men sat down, in number about five thousand. And Jesus took the loaves, and when He had given thanks He distributed them to the disciples, and the disciples to those sitting down; and likewise of the fish, as much as they wanted. So when they were filled, He said to His disciples, "Gather up the fragments that remain, so that nothing is lost." Therefore they gathered them up, and filled twelve baskets with the fragments of the five barley loaves which were left over by those who had eaten.

—*JOHN 6:5–13, NKJV*

God loves to surprise His children. As a result, He never tells a child all that He has planned for him.

I never dreamed that baseball would become the main consuming sport of my life during the next twenty-five years.

Because I was coaching girls' basketball, boys' hockey and boys' baseball, I was coaching year round. Both my oldest sister, Bernice, and my mother spoke to me before I was married and said the same thing: "You will not be able to coach as much as you have been now that you are getting married." I agreed with them.

We were all wrong. Because my wife's love of sports is even greater than mine, and perhaps because she is the better athlete, I ended up coaching more than ever.

When you are coaching teams that are not winning many games in a small village, there is not much pressure. However, the girls' basketball players were winning, and the hockey teams were becoming more competitive.

I had been involved with the executive duties of Ontario baseball. The opportunity arose for me to become its secretary registrar. This meant I would be the association's volunteer business manager. I sought this position and got it.

When I began, I needed an office secretary two or three days a month. I also needed two or three women to help in the office for six weeks in the busy summer. When I retired as the volunteer secretary registrar in 1992, I had two full-time employees working in our home office five days a week. In the summer, as many as seven people could be found working on Ontario baseball business.

Gwen Turner had come to work that first summer, and when I retired in 1992, she also retired as the first full-time employee of the association. She had become like a sister to our three children. Jamie felt that he could give Gwen orders in the office, but this never worked for him.

When I had become the secretary registrar, I felt I would retire from coaching. However, even though Jamie was only six years old, I told him that if he wanted to play baseball, I would work on developing a baseball program in Flesherton. If he wanted to play soccer, I would develop a soccer program. He chose baseball. I guess I wasn't thinking. There were people in our village who could coach soccer, but outside of Mr. Hill, who was seventy years old, who could coach baseball?

I had coached the past five summers at a town called Elmgrove. Jamie played his first baseball on this field, which had a cornfield as a fence line in right field. Elmgrove was just five miles from the Williams family farm, where we spent our summers. It was fun and relaxing, but the farm was being sold. So, we no longer had a place to go.

At the same time, Bob Elliott was leading the kinsman in the building of a baseball diamond for

Flesherton. I worked with Bob and became a member of Flesherton's baseball committee. Bob was a softball man. I was baseball through and through. We formed two baseball teams, with Mr. Hill working with the older team and myself working with the younger team. We played our first game in Midland. When we scored our first run, you would have thought we had won the World Series. That wasn't quite true, as the final score was 43-1 Midland.

In our first two years, we won a total of three games. In some ways, this was OK with me because it was a rest from long winning seasons in basketball and hockey.

Baseball would become our second son's sport. Rob always loved a ball. When we were in our first Ontario finals in 1983, Rob played in the outfield as a nine-year-old to give us nine players. In 1985, Rob was a member of Flesherton's first Ontario championship team. For me, it was an Ontario baseball championship team after having coached baseball for twenty-nine years. Between 1985 and 1996, Flesherton would win eighteen Ontario championships and have another thirteen teams reach the Ontario finals. This is an average of almost three teams a year playing in the Ontario finals.

It had become the biggest dynasty of all.

I served as president of the Flesherton ball association from 1979 to 1998. As with hockey, we hosted five or six tournaments of our own but never scheduled a single tournament game on a Sunday. We also hosted many Ontario championship tournaments. Some games in these tournaments had to be played on a Sunday. Ontario baseball would have as many as forty-four championships taking place. All of the tournaments had games beginning early on Sunday morning. There was one exception. No game in the tournaments hosted by Flesherton ever began until close to 1 P.M.

To God be the glory!

One final word on the hockey and baseball dynasties of Flesherton: Between 1979 and 1998, Flesherton had a total of fifty-six teams that have been either Ontario champions or finalists. That is almost an average of three teams a year for twenty years. Flesherton is still a village of fewer than seven hundred people.

Rob loved baseball so much that he decided to go to Arizona after high school as a "walk-on" at a junior college. We had visited Arizona five years earlier because I always was fascinated with Phoenix. It was not long before we bought a condo in Scottsdale. Rob and I went down after his high school graduation to visit various junior colleges in the Phoenix area, as well as Arizona State University and the University of Arizona. He chose Scottsdale College, which was less than fifteen minutes from our condo.

On our family's first visit to the city, we had attended Phoenix First Assembly because we saw its ad in the paper. There were special meetings at the church the week that Rob and I were there. We heard Tim Storey's sermon on being molded by the Master of molding.

When Rob returned to go to school in Scottsdale, he also chose to attend Phoenix First Assembly. He had visited two or three other churches but always went back there.

The first year at Scottsdale found Rob being redshirted. Coach Smith loved the attitude of this rather small, thin kid from Canada who had brains and didn't know enough to quit. The second year at the school, Rob was the last player chosen for the team. Coach Smith could not find it in his heart to cut him. In the fall of his third year, Rob was beginning to develop as a player. He was disappointed that he was not given a starting position.

In the second exhibition game, the starting catcher broke his toe in a freak accident at home plate. Rob became the starting catcher. When the other catcher came back, Rob and he equally shared the position.

There was a new coach at Southern California College in Costa Mesa who was building a ball program. Rob needed a place to play his final two years of school. Rob received a 75 percent scholarship to the college, divided between baseball and academics.

In his last year at Southern California, Rob was named NAIA Western United States Catcher of the Year. He was honorable mention for the national title. He was the school's Male Athlete of the Year. He is now an assistant coach of the team.

Like his brother, Rob accepted Jesus as his Savior beside his bed in prayer when he was a small boy. Before his tenth birthday, he was baptized in water at a Benny Hinn meeting in Ontario. He had walked with Jesus his entire life. He met Angela Minor while a student at Southern California. They got married in the summer of 1999. Angela walks as closely with the Lord as Rob does.

Although Rob hasn't had much money, his tithe for the past three years has gone to the Los Angeles International Church, where he has attended as a once-a-month guest.

CHAPTER 26

TROUBLED WATERS

*I will show you what he is like who comes to me
and hears my words and puts them into practice.
He is like a man building a house, who dug down
deep and laid the foundation on rock. When a
flood came, the torrent struck that house but could
not shake it, because it was well built. But the one
who hears my words and does not put them into
practice is like a man who built a house on the
ground without a foundation. The moment the
torrent struck that house, it collapsed and its
destruction was complete.*

—LUKE 6:47–49

In 1979, the ministerial fellowship in the Flesherton
area invited Marney Patterson to come to Grey
Highland for a week of crusade meetings. Months
of preparation went into the coming event. I had agreed
to be the co-chair of the event, along with our Baptist
minister. It was a success.

As a follow-up, a group called the South East Grey Praise Fellowship was formed. The executive team was a group of men who had been influenced in their growth in Christ by the crusade. The fellowship had representatives from many area churches.

The fellowship held monthly meetings on Sunday nights at St. John's United Church. At this time, only one church in the area was holding a regular Sunday evening service.

During the first couple of years, the monthly meetings often filled the church. A number of people committed and recommitted their lives to Christ.

As time passed, the people at the meetings became predictable. Altar calls had little meaning. The unsaved were not being invited to the meetings. The meetings began to die.

Reverend Wally Leeman shocked many of us with his sudden resignation from our church. He felt he needed to go elsewhere. He was replaced by a minister who was not sure what he believed or why he believed it. A number of families who had recent experiences with Jesus left our church. By mutual agreement, this minister soon decided to leave our community.

Reverend Don Prince came to town. He was a good speaker. He had personal charisma and was open to the charismatic teachings. St. John's United began to grow again.

There were several theological issues that the United Church of Canada began to discuss. The people within our church became concerned about many of these issues, even though they had no direct effect on St. John's.

Then came the issue of ordaining homosexuals. This issue became the straw that broke the camel's back. A number of people from St. John's decided to split and form a new church. Reverend Don Prince was one of the people.

I was chairman of the board at that time. In fact, I chaired a meeting one evening in which I knew that the new church was going to be formed at another meeting upon the close of the St John's congregational meeting.

There was no question where our family stood on the issue. Sin is sin. We must love the sinner but hate the sin. The question for us was where did God want us? We had spent our entire life proclaiming the gospel in the United Church. Jesus was criticized for eating with sinners. How can people be reached if there is not a messenger for Jesus?

We stayed. Most of the evangelicals in the church left. I have never been so criticized in my life as I was in the next few months by many of the area's evangelicals.

We lost all the Sunday school staff except one person. I was led to return to being superintendent of the Sunday school. Two days after the split, we had a complete staff in place. Although there were only twenty-seven people in church the following Sunday, the Sunday school attendance that day was close to 70 percent of what it had been.

During the coming years, I would have the opportunity of helping to proclaim the gospel to a new generation of people.

CHAPTER 27

STACEY

Then Jesus answered, "Woman, you have great faith! Your request is granted." And her daughter was healed from that very hour.
                                        —*MATTHEW 15:28*

O ur third child, Stacey, was born May 16, 1979. Both Father and Mother were full of thanksgiving that God had blessed us with a girl.

I guess I believed girls were born perfect. I have always placed women on pedestals. I was taught that women are special. I believe it. Yes, my wife also has her own little "ivory tower." As a result, I figured that Stacey would not have to be disciplined. This quickly changed.

It had not been difficult for me to give the two boys to the Lord. It was the natural and normal thing to do.

But I did have trouble giving Stacey to the Lord. When she was just a few months old, she became sick with a virus. Her body was almost completely limp. I went out of our home and circled it while praying and meditating. I gave my daughter up to the Lord. Within hours, the flu had left her.

A few years later, we were at Phoenix First Assembly for the first time. Pastor Tommy Barnett gave the altar call. After half a minute, I realized that Stacey was tugging on my sleeve. I was surprised. I believed that she had committed her life as a small girl much like her brothers.

I asked her if she wanted to go to the altar. She said yes because she wasn't sure that she had accepted Jesus. She went, and she accepted her Savior.

In the months that followed, I came to realize that this was a life-changing experience for our daughter. She had been the most rebellious child that we had. This nature disappeared after that night.

Rob was attending school in Scottsdale. I was getting ready to retire. Stacey was a freshman in high school. I wondered if she might be interested in going to school in Arizona. I had the month of January off. Stacey went to Phoenix for two weeks with Rob, Jason Neil and me.

On the Sunday evening, Pastor Tommy Barnett presented his illustrated sermon "The Rebounder," using basketball to illustrate it. Stacey rededicated her life and was baptized that evening. Jason Neil accepted the Lord as Savior and also was baptized.

Stacey decided to go to school in Phoenix. She attended Xavier Catholic school for the next two years. The academic standards were great. Stacey found the contrast of the theology classes at Xavier and at First Assembly to be a challenge. It helped her faith grow. Besides being a regular member of Brad Baker's youth group at the church, she also was involved in a discipleship group for young people.

For her final year of secondary school, she chose to go to Scottsdale Christian Academy. Like her brothers, Stacey possessed some good athletic ability. She led her team to the 1A state semifinals in basketball. She won a state championship in track in the hurdles. As a younger girl, she and her partner received a bronze medal in their Canadian division of novice pairs skating. They qualified for the Eastern Canadian Divisional Championships.

After completing secondary school, Stacey was accepted to become a student of the Master's Commission under Lloyd Zeigler at Phoenix First Assembly. Stacey is now a staff member of Master's Commission.

CHAPTER 28

SLOVAKIA

No one serving as a soldier gets involved in civilian affairs—he wants to please his commanding officer.

—2 TIMOTHY 2:4

I n the 1980s, the state of Czechoslovakia became divided into the Czech Republic and Slovakia.

I had received a phone call from Terry Slobodian, who worked for the missionary group Navigators. He was interested in starting baseball in Slovakia, and some folks in Ontario had referred him to me. The Communist regimes of Eastern Europe had not allowed baseball because they associated it with capitalism. But since Communism had disappeared, baseball was now allowed.

I met with Terry to talk about baseball in Slovakia. He needed used equipment, uniforms, gloves, balls and bats. Slovakia didn't even have a baseball diamond. I offered to help get him some equipment. He was hoping that I would go to Slovakia and put on baseball clinics, something I had done in Ontario.

I personally did not do these things any longer, but a group of ten boys from Flesherton, with our son Jamie in charge, did. I was just the organizer. I suggested to Terry that some of the boys go over.

I worked with Terry in getting contacts for the organization, which he called Good Sports. We talked about doing come clinics in Slovakia but didn't at that time. However, Terry had other contacts that did provide clinics.

As part of my retirement in 1994, my wife and I went on a trip to England, Scotland, France, Switzerland and Slovakia. Slovakia was to be a one-week working part of the trip. I did conduct some baseball clinics then, one of which was to introduce college students to baseball. I helped Terry with a couple of team practices, as well as a Bible study.

The mission principle of Navigators is to win people one by one and disciple them.

While in Slovakia, Terry took us to the largest high-rise in Eastern Europe, where more than six hundred thousand people live. It is part of the great historical city of Bratislava. Even though it is a large community, it has no church. It was built by the Communists.

Terry told us there was a teenage dance held in the high-rise that fall. After the dance, more than one thousand syringes were found on the dance hall floor. The leaders of Bratislava called it "a sociological disaster waiting to happen."

I came home from Slovakia with a major burden for Petrozalko. Navigators could never work fast enough to bring revival to help these kids. Something more was needed. I thought about the young people from Flesherton going to Slovakia and spending a summer. But this didn't happen. My burden for Slovakia continued.

After coming home from Slovakia, I experienced my first Tommy Barnett Pastor's School. I thought it would be a good idea for Terry to come to the next Pastor's School. But he didn't.

Another year went by. The burden of Slovakia continued to be part of me.

I told Terry that if he could arrange for one or two people to come to Pastor's School in 1997, we would pay the travel expenses. It was at Pastor's School in 1996 that the Lord helped me to realize that a group from Flesherton would have no idea how to deal with the inner-city problems of Bratislava. However, a team from Master's Commission from First Assembly would have some ideas.

Terry arranged for Iveta to come to Pastor's School.

Iveta was a quiet young woman from a small, conservative evangelical church whose membership was fewer than twenty. Iveta and her husband were the only members younger than fifty years old. Iveta, who has a problem with her ears, learned her broken English from Terry and his wife.

We went to the first Pastor's School meeting. Iveta had never been involved with such crowds, and the volume of praise hurt her ears.

After the first day, I asked, "Lord, what is this all about? Why is Iveta here? How does she fit in?"

Iveta stayed until school was over. During her last day in Phoenix, we talked about her responsibility when she went home.

Her church could not help. But what could she do? She told me her brother-in-law attended a First Assembly Church in Bratislava. She would tell him about the Master's Commission. Maybe he could help.

In the meantime, I had talked to Lloyd Zeigler about the Master's Commission going to Slovakia. He was open to the idea. I introduced him to Iveta.

When Iveta returned to Slovakia, she contacted her brother-in-law, who contacted his pastor. Pastor Latko was interested.

I called Pastor Latko. He said his daughter had spent a year in the Master's Commission in Seattle. It turns out they had been praying for two years that the Master's Commission would come to Bratislava. He said he never dreamed that the original Master's Commission from Phoenix would come to the city.

In May 1998, a team from Master's Commission, including our daughter, went to Bratislava to minister.

What an awesome God we serve—to think that the Holy Spirit would arrange for a man from Canada to go to Slovakia about baseball so he would develop a burden for that country and contact Master's Commission, which would go help Slovakia in an answer to prayer!

One more little fact: I thought it was mainly me until I discovered that God was completely in control, as He always is.

CHAPTER 29

PHOENIX FIRST ASSEMBLY

"Give, and it will be given to you. A good measure,
pressed down, shaken together and running over,
will be poured into your lap. For with the measure
you use, it will be measured to you.

—LUKE 6:38

I have been fascinated with Phoenix since I was a young boy. It was fascination that brought our family in the late 1980s to see the land of my childhood cowboy heroes. We quickly fell in love with the land.

But I had never heard of Phoenix First Assembly or Tommy Barnett until I saw the ad in the *Arizona Republic*. It was with difficulty that we got to the far side of the city to eventually find Cave Creek. We entered the church at the second balcony level. Several white buses were arriving. People were being fed just inside the door. We chose to move down to the first floor for our first service.

As with Arizona, it was instant love. Our daughter accepted Jesus that night.

I could not return to Phoenix without returning to Phoenix First Assembly. Eventually, that was reversed. I wanted to get to Phoenix in order to get to the church. For the past decade, I have been involved as a "trench warrior" in this church during my time in Phoenix. Monday prayer from 6 to 7 A.M. is a regular part of my schedule. Sunday morning and evening are worship times. Wednesday evening offers prayer and Bible study.

During one fall, I cleaned the buses for Jeff Allaway. I traveled on a few of them. I fell in love with the effort of Raymond Kellogg, a former bus boy who is now the leader of the sidewalk bus ministry. I watched Bernie Cull as he continued his amazing witness to people while he took care of his wife, who was battling Alzheimer's, and the genius of David Ritter, and the piano player who is always there. I watched Leo's faithfulness. Brad Baker became special as he ministered to our daughter. I quickly came to call Dale Lane "Andrew." There is always a need for an "Andrew" to work behind the scenes for a "Peter," and Dale has filled that role quite well on behalf of Pastor Tommy Barnett.

In recent years, I have had the opportunity to help out with Master's Commission while becoming an admirer of the efforts of the director, Lloyd Zeigler.

And what about the Los Angeles International Church? Since Rob has been in Costa Mesa, California, my wife and I have had many opportunities to visit that church. We have watched it grow. We have watched its amazing outreach. It, too, has become part of us.

CHAPTER 30

DADDY, LIFT ME HIGHER

There he found some disciples and asked them, "Did you receive the Holy Spirit when you believed?" They answered, "No, we have not even heard that there is a Holy Spirit." So Paul asked, "Then what baptism did you receive?" "John's baptism," they replied. Paul said, "John's baptism was a baptism of repentance. He told the people to believe in the one coming after him, that is, in Jesus." On hearing this, they were baptized into the name of the Lord Jesus. When Paul placed his hands on them, the Holy Spirit came on them, and they spoke in tongues and prophesied.

—ACTS 19:1–6

Flesherton is still our home. We are still members of St. John's United Church. In 1998, I coached our senior baseball team, which had four players who played in that 43-1 loss in Midland in the 1970s.

The senior team was quite different. It had lost 2-1 to the defending Ontario champions from Toronto.

I coached the two girls' basketball teams from Grey Highlands for the first time in five years. The junior girls went to CWOSSA. It was the first girls' basketball team to go to CWOSSA in five years. I served as chairman of the board of management of St. John's Church.

The Los Angeles International Church is one of the outreach missions of St. John's. Just a few years ago, St. John's was in debt. The church had operated for a number of years under a deficit. During that year, LAIC became part of St. John's mission outreach. In November and December of that year, the church's finances experienced a turnaround. The church's budget finished with a surplus. Since then, the church has had a surplus every year.

On Thanksgiving 1998, St. John's had its first out-reach dinner. The church of one hundred fifty-two members provided a free Thanksgiving meal to one hundred twenty people. In addition, another $700 was distributed to feed those in need. The first verse of Psalm 41 says, "Blessed is he that considereth the poor: the LORD will deliver him in time of trouble" (KJV).

The Master's Commission came to Grey County, where group members led ten school assemblies, held special rallies, provided a training seminar for forty people and led in worship at four church services. The team ministered to more than four thousand people in ten days. On a Saturday night, more than three hundred young people rushed to the school stage when asked, "Do you want more of God?" I also went to the altar. I had seen the drive and the enthusiasm of the Master's kids, but especially of my daughter. I wanted more of God. Junior prayed for me.

Six members of the Master's Commission returned to Flesherton for three weeks in July to disciple twenty-five of our youth. They led worship at St. John's Vacation Bible School, which has been an outreach of St. John's for more than twenty years. More than one hundred fifty people participated in Vacation Bible School in 1998. Street outreach meetings were held in Dundalk. The team led a major rally on the shores of Georgian Bay for a holiday crowd at the beach.

More than thirty people have come to Phoenix First Assembly from the Flesherton area for at least one worship service. Illustrated sermons are becoming part of the regular menu in many Flesherton area churches.

Well, that's the story of this grizzled old trench warrior. But God isn't finished with me yet! He has more for me to do! What does the future hold? I have no idea. But I know the One who holds the future, and He is full of surprises! And I am certain that all my tomorrows will be blessed as I walk in His Spirit.

I begin each day with a simple prayer: "Good morning, Holy Spirit, my Senior Partner! Make today an exciting day for You in my life!" That is my prayer because I know that if it is an exciting day for the Father's beloved Holy Spirit, who loves Jesus so much, it will also be an exciting day for me.

And that's really what it is all about. Jesus must increase, and I must decrease. It must all be to God's glory, because when it is, it will also be His best for me.

"Daddy, in the name of Your Son, please lift me higher by doing Your perfect will in my life. And I pray the same for the readers of this book. May each one discover and experience the privilege and adventure of being a trench warrior for You. Thank You, in Jesus' wonderful name, for sending Your Holy Spirit to comfort, teach, guide, equip and empower *all* Your trench warriors!"

EPILOGUE

TRIBUTES TO GOD'S FAITHFULNESS

For great is your love, reaching to the heavens; your faithfulness reaches to the skies. Be exalted, O God, above the heavens; let your glory be over all the earth.

—PSALM 57:10–11

TEACHER OF THE MONTH

The Teacher of the Month of January is Mr. Pegg. He was born in Beeton, Ontario. Now he lives across the street from the school in Highland Heights. Before teaching at our school, he taught at Alliston for four years and at Newmarket for six years.

His favorite food is hot dogs–anybody's hot dogs; he isn't fussy.

He'd like to coach the Detroit Red Wings to the

Stanley Cup. He doesn't consider young people brats; he loves kids. He teaches history and coaches the senior girls' basketball team. (That's probably why they did so well.)

Mr. Pegg, whose first name is Ron, doesn't like to yell, but sometimes he feels it is necessary. He just yells at the individual, not the whole class.

He was Wayne Carleton's (now with the California Seals) first coach. He was also Jim Rutherfud's coach. Jim is now with Pittsburgh.

He graduated from Waterloo Lutheran University, and just last week, he was informed that he had received a master's degree in education from Toronto. Congratulations on that.

The most important thing in Mr. Pegg's life is the love that Jesus Christ has for him. It is because of his love that Mr. Pegg came here. In other words, Mr. Pegg feels that Christ wanted him to come here.

Congratulations on being the Teacher of the Month. We hope you will stay and teach at Grey Highlands for many years to come.

—Regina Remisch
Grey Highlands Student Newspaper, January 1972

RAMBLINGS FROM GRANDPA'S ARMCHAIR

There is a hockey practice scheduled for today. There is a hockey game scheduled for tomorrow. For the game, you can be almost positive that everyone will be there who possibly can. For the practice, everyone may be there, but someone probably will be absent. A family has gone shopping. It is OK to miss practice for shopping, but do not miss the game! Someone has a touch of the flu. Someone has a headache or a toothache. The person is not sick enough to miss a game, but he misses practice. The game is canceled because the other team cannot come. Some people who miss the practice would have come to the game.

The ideas of our society say the game can't be missed, but it is OK not to practice. How wrong we are! The practice is, in most cases, more important than the game. It is in practice that we learn the basics. In fact, without practice, it is a farce to play.

I have watched players practice only a slap shot during practice or pre-game warm-up. Then I have watched the same people play the game. In the entire game, they never get a slap shot, which hits the net. Of course, they don't score.

You see, one person out of about thirty or forty can effectively use a slap shot. What a waste of time to practice the slap shot when it has little or no use to the person who is practicing it. A few years ago, many kids would practice a hook shot in basketball. They would shoot it half the time, and the chance of it going in during a game were slim. Like the slap shot, the hook shot is beautiful and exciting to watch when it works, but these shots are not basics for the game. Gordie Howe, who has scored more goals than anyone else in the history of the NHL, never scored even one goal with a slap shot.

It is important for us to realize that we must practice the right things.

This is the beginning point for all of us in everything we do. We must work at the right basics to succeed. To run, a child must first creep, then walk, then run. It takes a lot of practice to reach the stage where you can run.

You must practice the right basics, and then, when the time comes to run, you will be able to run.

To succeed in life, the first basic is Jesus Christ.

—Ron Pegg
(a weekly column written by Ron Pegg)
The Flesherton Advance, April 1982

The South East Grey Praise Fellowship

Under the auspices of the Praise Fellowship, Ernie Hollands ministered to a responsive audience at Grey Highlands Secondary School on Friday evening, April 2. Friends were noted from Owen Sound, Horning's Mills, Shelburne and more. In charge of the meeting was Jim Green of Flesherton, with Paul Stewart of Dundalk the song leader, and Ellen Armstrong. Marjorie McIntyre ministered in song, accompanied by Heather Wright.

Ernie, as he prefers to be known, is a dynamic and forceful speaker. Telling of his birth in the slums of Halifax, taught by his mother to steal when he was eight years old, Ernie knew nothing else of most of his young life. Theft, bank robbery, even attempted murder, contributed to his record of twenty-five years in various jails.

Finally, in Millhaven Maximum Security Penitentiary, a Christian businessman wrote to him, visited him, loved him and gave him a Bible. Ernie began to pray for help. To hear him tell of how Christ visited him in his cell, of how he saw Jesus and heard him say, "Ernie, your slate is wiped clean" is a thrilling testimony to the power of Jesus to recreate a human personality. Today, he travels far and wide, telling his story of the kindness, grace and power of the living Lord, who is able to make all of us into "new creatures in Jesus Christ."

In the afternoon, Ernie was pleased to have the privilege of addressing students at an assembly at Grey Highlands Secondary School.

—Ellen Armstrong
The Flesherton Advance, 1982

FLESHERTON'S FIRST ONTARIO HOCKEY CHAMPIONSHIP

The Flesherton Joe's Service Station Peewees ended their reach for the Ontario Championship with an impressive 10-2 win over Douro on Sunday, April 4, 1982. The win gave the team a sweep of its three-game championship series. The series wins gave the Peewees a playoff record of twelve wins and one tie. It climaxed a season in which the team won twenty-seven league and playoff games, while tying one game and losing one game when less than half of the regular team was there on a snowy night in December.

This team won the OMHA regional championship in Atom D&E two years ago with a 28-0 record. (In Atom, the regional championship is the furthest a team can go.) As a result, this team has had a record of fifty-five wins, one loss and one tie while winning the championship. The team scored two hundred ninety-four goals while having fifty-nine scored against it. This means that the team averaged 10.1 goals a game and 2.04 goals a game scored against it.

In Sunday's championship final, Flesherton went ahead 1-0 in the first period as the Douro goalie, Mike Meade, stopped more than twenty shots, six of which were hard to handle. In the second period, the Flesherton team finally found the range and rifled home seven goals to go ahead 8-0. In the third period, the teams split four goals to make the final count 10-2 for the champs.

Earlier Games

In earlier games in the series, the Joe's Service Station boys won 6-3 in Douro in the opening game and 6-1 at home on Saturday. In the first game, team captain Scott Betts was the scoring star with five goals, while Dan Neil added one. Flesherton led 3-1 after the first period and 5-2 at the end of the second. In Saturday's game, Mike Meade, the Douro goalie, carried his team on his shoulder for two periods. The score was tied 1-1 with seven seconds to go in the second period when Betts gave the hometown boys a 2-1 lead. Flesherton then scored four times in the last period to win 6-1. Chris Chapman starred with the hat trick, while Betts added two and Neil added one.

In Sunday's final game, the balance of this team showed itself, as eleven players figured in the scoring. Richard Davidson scored two while picking up an assist. Betts scored twice and had three assists. Dan Harrison scored twice, Mike Tsimidis scored once and added three assists, and Neil, Scott Sutter and Paul Stoddart each scored once. Jason Pate and Jamie Pegg picked up assists. Colin MacMillan played the first two periods of shutout goaltending, while Zeldk Zkeric played in the net the last period. Chapman and Billy Carson also played steady hockey in this championship contest. Both players had good shots on goal that Meade stopped.

The championship marks the first Ontario championship in the history of Flesherton.

The boys are to be congratulated on winning the championship and doing it in such a convincing manner.

The team will be honored with a ride around town on the fire engine this Saturday afternoon.

–Sports column
The Flesherton Advance, April 1982

FLESHERTON'S FIRST ONTARIO BASEBALL CHAMPIONSHIP

With only ten Peewee players, the Flesherton Split Railers won the All Ontario Peewee E championship in the tournament in Sutton on Labor Day weekend.

The team earlier had won the Red Henry tournament in July in Walkerton. The tournament is for teams in Western Ontario. The team also finished on top of the league with a record nine wins and three losses. Other teams in the league were Walkerton, Listowel and Kincardine. Hanover entered the league, but later withdrew.

Flesherton had to play Dashwood for the right to go to the Ontario championships. The team played a double-header in Dashwood, defeating the hometown crew 10-0 and 11-0 as Mark Brodie and Jeremy Franks both threw shutout baseball for the Split Railers.

In the first game in Sutton, Flesherton jumped upon the Langton pitching for three quick runs. However, Langton tied the score after four innings. In the top of the fifth, Flesherton scored five runs to take an 8-3 lead. Brodie did not allow another run, and Flesherton won 8-3.

In game two, Flesherton again came out fast with two runs. A long double by Dillon Fremlin was the big hit in the fourth inning, as this hit drove in two runs. Jeremy Franks allowed single runs in the first and third innings, but shut out Moraviantown, which is near Chatham, for the rest of the game, and Flesherton won 5-2.

Robbie Pegg starred at short stop in game three. He threw out seven runners at first base. Flesherton only had four hits, but Brodie only allowed Sutton three hits. A triple by Todd Davis scored two runs in the fourth, and Flesherton won 6-2.

This victory put Flesherton into the finals.

Langton was Flesherton's opponent again the second game. (Langton had remained undefeated since playing Flesherton in the first game of this double-elimination tournament.)

However , a tired Langton team was no opposition for the high-flying Split Railers. The team scored two runs in the first inning, which would have been enough for Jeremy Franks, who threw a two-hit shutout. Seven runs in the top of the fourth, highlighted by Brodie's three-run triple, made the score 10-0. Flesherton won the championship 11-0.

–Sports column
The Flesherton Advance, September 1985

Epilogue

Scottsdale Christian's Pegg Sparks Quarterfinal Victory

Scottsdale Christian Academy's Stacey Pegg had trouble with traveling violations early in the season and was just beginning to develop her jump shot.

On Thursday in the Class 1A girls' state tournament, though, she became the most unlikely of stars.

Pegg moved quite nicely and avoided the pinstriped cops at the same time to lead Scottsdale to a 57-29 win over defending state champion Northwest Community Christian at America West Arena.

Scottsdale (18-6) will face St. Michael's (19-6), a 38-31 winner over Fort Thomas, in the semifinals at 11:45 A.M. today at America West Arena.

In the other first round games, Salone (19-7) beat Arizona Lutheran (20-5) 40-36, and St. David (17-7) defeated Mogollon (10-11) 56-36.

Salone will play St. David at 8:15 A.M. today at America West Arena.

Pegg got Scottsdale started with two quick baskets, an assist to Julie Van Weelden and a steal she took the length of the floor for two, staking the Eagles to an 8-4 lead they never relinquished.

"We had to come out with a lot of intensity, and I just wanted to hit my shots from the beginning," Pegg said. "I like to bug the other team, frustrate them by getting a hand on a pass or by putting on pressure."

Pegg had four steals, all leading to points, and had sixteen points, the most she's ever scored. Her previous high was eight.

"She's very quick and aggressive," Scottsdale Coach Bob Fredericks said. "At the beginning of the year, she really didn't have a jump shot. But she's put a lot of work into getting her feet right and shooting."

In the Salone victory, Mary Ahart had nine of her twenty-three points in the third quarter. The win avenged two earlier losses to Arizona Lutheran.

"Mary is really our key," Salone Coach Dan Wolfe said. "She really stepped up. She had what it takes."

Celest Perez hit the go-ahead basket with twenty-eight seconds left, and Ahart iced the win with a drive down the lane.

—Kenny Tomb
Special for *The Republic*, February 29, 1997

COACHING CAREER STARTED IN STANDS

Flesherton—In Ron Pegg's high school basketball coaching debut, he sat with the spectators.

He perched in the stands across from his team's bench in a Newmarket gymnasium, using hand signals to tell his players what to do.

It was 1965, and Pegg had been persuaded by his wife, Cathy, the Newmarket school's physical education teacher, to coach the senior girls' basketball team.

It was the first year of a dramatic rule change that opened up girls' hoops and brought it on the same footing, style-wise, to what boys were playing.

But a man wasn't allowed to coach girls' basketball.

Epilogue

Pegg could run the practices and scrimmages, but during games, he had to hand-signal what he wanted his team to do from a distance.

The next year, he was allowed to sit on the bench. But he couldn't talk directly to the referees. He had to tell his assistant coach what he wanted to say. She'd relay it to the officials.

Five years later, Pegg moved to Grey Highland in Flesherton. He coached his seniors to the Central Western district championships, but a rival coach objected.

According to the district rules, it still was illegal for a man to coach. But the next year, the district changed its mind.

"I was beginning to feel like a pioneer in a way," Pegg said with a laugh as he recounted the tale.

Fast-forward to 1993, and Pegg, fifty-six, is still coaching girls' basketball.

But this winter, he's hanging up his high-tops.

And his skates.

And his chalk and brushes. He's retiring from Grey Highland, too.

After nearly forty years of coaching hockey, baseball and basketball, Pegg is calling it quits.

"You could say coaching has been my full-time hobby. I coach year round," Pegg said.

He still plans on being involved in baseball—the sport he's coached the longest and the sport in which he won a provincial Volunteer of the Year award—but probably only from an organizational standpoint.

Pegg adds that surprisingly, he won't miss bench bossing. "Maybe baseball during a warm summer," the affable history teacher said with a chuckle.

Pegg has been so successful in his basketball coaching career that the Central Western district retired its championship trophy to Grey Highland. Pegg and his Lions teams had won it so often..

Pegg often coached both the junior and senior teams the same year.

He's been to the districts twenty-five times, been in the finals nineteen times and won thirteen titles.

Starting in 1974, his team won eight straight divisional championships. During that period, he also coached the senior team to five divisional titles.

"Often that meant that I'd finish coaching a senior game, then coach a junior game, then coach a senior game, then coach a—Phew," he said. "I was younger then."

This winter, his senior Lions lost the Grey County final but went on to the districts on the strength of a Grey-Bruce crossover win. No district title this year.

Now that basketball season is over, he's moved on to a local Atom hockey squad—the 190th team he's coached.

But basketball is his favorite sport. He likes the instantaneous strategy and the way the game continues to evolve.

But his philosophy about the game, which sums up his coaching philosophy in general, hasn't changed.

"My philosophy is play because you want to," Pegg said.

"Life begins with basketball, it doesn't end with it."

—Don Harrison, Sports Writer
(Written about Ron Pegg's retirement from teaching)
The Owen Sound Sun Times, December 1993

Epilogue

Ron Pegg Retires

An OBA era has ended as Ron Pegg, in December, advised the OBA board of his desire to retire from active responsibilities. In the history of the OBA, Ron, an honorary member, occupies a foremost position among our most important contributors.

Space prevents detailing all of his contributions to baseball in a career spanning about forty years. Ron began coaching in Beeton, where he was one of the organizers of the local system in the 1950s. From there, he moved to Flesherton and was founder of the Flesherton minor baseball program, which has prospered through the ensuing years enjoying great success in OBA competition.

Ron chaired the founding meeting of the York Simcoe Baseball Association, served as its first president for four years and then as secretary and registrar for two more years. In 1969, Ron was York Simcoe's first appointee to the OBA board. In 1976, he was an elected board member and was appointed secretary, treasurer and registrar, a position he held for fifteen years. These years marked an explosion in the growth of amateur baseball. There were just five hundred registered teams in the OBA when Ron started as secretary with the part-time help of Gwen Turner, who, a few years later, became our first permanent staff person.

Ron started this newsletter in 1979 on a few photocopied sheets of paper. He served as editor until last year. The OBA's first computer was purchased for the office in Ron's basement, not that he ever dared to touch it! OBA business became a family affair as Cathy, Jamie, Rob and Stacey answered the busy telephone. In his spare time, Ron "worked" as a high school teacher, achieving an exceptional coaching record there as well with the girls' basketball teams.

Ron started the participation development clinics in 1987 as an outreach program to areas of the province where baseball was new or non-existent. The clinics have contributed greatly to the growth of our game, particularly in North Ontario due to the efforts of Ron and his colleagues.

Ron Pegg was a primary leader in the development of both rookie ball and girls' baseball. His untiring promotion of these programs has led to their inclusion in the OBA.

Now retired from teaching, Ron spends much of the year in Scottsdale, Arizona, returning to Flesherton for the baseball season (after the snow melts). Ron and Cathy stay busy keeping track of their brood, Jamie in Calgary, Rob in California and Stacey in Arizona. Sports continue to play a major role in the Peggs' lives as the kids have inherited Ron's talent and love for sports (or is it Cathy's talent?).

We are sure that everyone involved in baseball in Ontario joins us in thanking Ron for his years of dedicated service and in wishing him and his family well. God bless.

—Howie Birnie, OBA Past President
(Written about Ron Pegg's Retirement from active involvement with Ontario baseball)
Baseball Bits, April 1996

To contact the author

Write to: Ron Pegg
              P.O. Box 213
              Flesherton, Ontario N0C 1E0

Or e-mail: erpegg@bmts.com